BONE ROSARY

ALSO BY THOMAS LYNCH

POETRY

Skating with Heather Grace
Grimalkin & Other Poems
Still Life in Milford
Walking Papers
The Sin-Eater: A Breviary

NONFICTION

The Undertaking: Life Studies from the Dismal Trade
Bodies in Motion and at Rest: On Metaphor and Mortality
Booking Passage: We Irish and Americans
The Good Funeral (with Thomas G. Long)
Whence and Whither: A Miscellany
The Depositions: New and Selected Essays

FICTION

Apparition & Late Fictions

BONE ROSARY

New and Selected Poems

THOMAS LYNCH

Godine

❧ BOSTON 2021 ❧

Published in 2021 by
Godine
Boston, Massachusetts

LIBRARY OF CONGRESS CATALOGING-IN-PUBLICATION DATA
Names: Lynch, Thomas, 1948- author.
Title: Bone rosary : new and selected poems / Thomas Lynch.
Description: Boston, Massachusetts : David R. Godine, Publisher, [2021]
Identifiers: LCCN 2020038789 (print) | LCCN 2020038790 (ebook)
ISBN 9781567927016 (hardcover)
ISBN 9781567927023 (ebook)
Subjects: LCGFT: Poetry.
Classification: LCC PS3562.Y437 B66 2021 (print) | LCC PS3562.Y437
   (ebook) | DDC 811/.54--dc23
LC record available at https://lccn.loc.gov/2020038789
LC ebook record available at https://lccn.loc.gov/2020038790

FIRST PRINTING, 2021
Printed in the United States of America

This book is for
The Tata Sisters,
Julie and Mary,
without whom nothing
give them their due.

And in memory of
my daughter,
Heather Grace,
1975–2020

CONTENTS

※ *from* GRIMALKIN & OTHER POEMS

※ *from* STILL LIFE IN MILFORD

꙳ *from* WALKING PAPERS

The big dog's grave is already dug, a few
yards from the lake, and all the bones he's
sucked the marrow from are strung on a rope
draped over the porch railing, a bone rosary,
waiting to be hooked to a rusty chain hung
from a metal post stuck in the ground, poking
over the water.

from "The Bone Rosary" in *On Mullett Lake,* 2017
Matthew Sweeney (1952–2018)

CLOUD OF WITNESSES

An Introduction

I STARTED STRINGING soup bones on a rope, for reasons I'm not entirely sure of, ten years ago. My old dog, Bill—the only mammal over a hundred pounds who could bide with me—was still alive, though well into his slow decrepitude, and the soup bones were a sort of compensation, a little bonus for his singular loyalty.

Bill had been named for a pair of *WW*'s: William Wordsworth and William Wilson, the former a poet and the latter a cofounder of a fellowship of drunks in pursuit of sobriety. "Call him Bill W.," my wife said, exasperated at my getting a dog over her objections. I was looking, as always, for a way to bridge the gaps, for metaphors, for a way to make it to the other side, a carrying across, from one being to another. I don't know. I was trying, I suppose, to connect the dots.

My wife and I were growing more distant; my sons were involved with lives of their own; and after two years of joint counseling, my daughter, Heather Grace, had made known her rejection of her "family of origin," of which I was the patriarch. I was trying to reestablish connections, trying to find a way back into the Rockwell print of a family gathering around a common table, a turkey dinner and giving thanks. Bill and I had removed ourselves to this house on the south end of a big lake in northern Michigan, half an hour south of the Straits of Mackinaw. Having survived the surgery to correct a broken heart—a stenotic aortic valve that left me breathless and enfeebled—I was determined to use what time and renewed energy that savagery bought me to get some writing done.

My sons told me I was "not retired but not required" at the funeral home that had been my life's work for more than forty years, so I should remain up north as long as I liked. In the past half decade, I haven't budged from here save for some travel, mostly for funerals, mostly to Ireland and the UK, where I still have interests and neighbors, or back home to Milford, Michigan, for the deaths of old friends. I'd hire a dog-sitter to pour kibble into Bill's bowl and offer him a bone from time to time. The butcher at the local grocery store would cut up a bag full of bones in inch-and-a-half circular portions, long femurs from beef cattle, and keep them in the freezer at the back of the store. I'd pick up a new bag every month. For his part, Bill took the bones in his gob like viaticum itself, then hurry off to the soft ground beneath the spreading sugar maple and lick and chew the bones clean of the fatty marrow at the core, which contained the essence of the bovine these bespoke servings were relics of. It calmed him, I suppose, the mouthy labor, the greasy treat, not to mention the aid to his aged bowels. Maybe it gave him dreams of bison or Black Angus herds munching the greensward and geography before humans fixed on such beasts with their carnivorous hunger. Hard to know.

When Bill's hips gave out, between his tenth and eleventh year, I doubled the daily dosage of bones, and they littered the lawn like hard SpaghettiOs by the time I shuffled around to pick them up, lest they be run over by a power mower and shot through a window or take out some unsuspecting human. I'd go around to Bill's usual haunts and gather the wee sun-bleached hollowed vowels, then string them on a rope stretched out on the big porch where I sat most days in agreeable weather to read or type. They clattered like an abacus when I moved them and I imagined they were keeping track of some strange arithmetic that was part calendar, part calculator, part primitive clock, by which I resolved to keep tethered to the passing of real time and higher purposes.

"What does it all mean?" I'd ask myself about the business of being and the gift of life, and the bone ropes became a sort of symbol of that query. However it calmed Bill to lick the marrow out of them, it calmed me, too, to see them lengthening with the advancing seasons and passing time, a snake of fragmented thoughts that sought, as notions do, some connection to the slithering and elusive meaning of things. Once the ropes got to a certain length, I'd have them hoisted up to hang from a fulcrum that over-arched the lake shallows where the former tenant of these premises had rigged a method, by tether and turnstile and countervailing weights, to shift the nose of his dock out into the lake where he kept his canoe and fishing boat. The dock is gone, the turnstile defunct, the counterweights disappeared, but the fulcrum remains—the vantage of rattling kingfisher birds and the drop for my hanging ropes and bones. The bone ropes gave purpose to the defunct fulcrum and in the giving gathered meaning unto themselves, however mysterious and provisional the meanings seemed.

IN THE AUTUMN of 2016, my friend the Irish poet Matthew Sweeney made his last trip to North America. Matthew was always willing to travel for poetry and kept body and soul together for years by his here-again-and-gone-tomorrow pilgrimage in service to his verse. When I made known to my friend Emily Meier, one of the organizers of the inaugural Harbor Springs Festival of the Book, that Matthew would be Stateside and in the neighborhood, she asked what it would take to get him to come to northern Michigan. I told her they could pay for his ticket and a respectable stipend and that he'd be welcome to stay with me on Mullett Lake, a place he'd visited several times in the 1990s. Emily obliged and an invitation was extended.

That October by the lake, Matthew and I sat on the porch and he eyed me lacing rope through some bones, old Bill stretched in repose at his feet. "For fook's sake, Lynch," he said, "what's that about?"

"About six more feet," I replied, "to add to the bone rosary, yonder," nodding toward the fulcrum at the edge of the water. I'd never said "bone rosary" before but noticed now how pleasant the sound of those long *o*'s were in the saying of them; and because I knew Matthew would still be wondering, I commenced on a narrative that might tickle his fantasies and imagination. I told him that living as I was, unarmed and in solitude, at the end of a dead end road off the beaten track, I would sometimes worry over home invasions from terrorists, local religious or political fanatics, and other malfeasants. I saw the bone rosary as a totem against the worst impulses of extremist pike fishermen and watersports jihadis. I thought that anyone getting a look at a bone rosary hanging over my water frontage would regard the resident of this demesne to be what clinicians call "crazier than a hoot-owl," and keep their distance accordingly. A man who hung soup bones on a rope and hung bundles of same over the edge of his lakefront from on high was clearly not the sort to be tampered with.

"And so far," I told Matthew, "it's working fine."

I did not tell him that something about the bone-covered rope, the way it hung from the fulcrum's nose, looped and insouciant, put me in mind of the fifteen-decade chain of black rosary beads I remember looped on the right hip of Sr. Jean Térèse— the bed of heaven to her—who tried to teach me the mysteries of life and love's bewilderments when I was a sixth-grader at Holy Name. More than anything she ever said, it was the lay of that rosary across her hip and nether regions, all of them draped in the deep blue habit of the Sister Servants of the Immaculate Heart of Mary, and the bump of her bottom and ample breasts under long scapular that covered those mysteries fore and aft, that made me aware of my wanting to know, with an urgency I did not understand, more about her. Was this the knowledge referred to in the book of Genesis that made Adam and Eve ashamed of their nakedness after they ate of the Forbidden Fruit? Not the knowledge of good and evil, rather the knowledge of the good and graceful, the gifts of "unabashed gratitude"—to borrow from the poet Ross Gay—the joy of beholding one another as we are.

"Nuns fret not at their convent's narrow rooms," wrote the other Bill W.—William Wordsworth—in a sonnet he wrote in praise of sonnets. In the confinement of the form he saw a freedom. The limit of lines, the count of syllables, the measure of meters, acoustics and rhymes, made the rummage through the word horde easier.

> *In sundry moods 'twas pastime to be bound*
> *Within the Sonnet's scanty plot of ground:*

Likewise, yet another Bill W.—William Carlos Williams—often focused on the unadorned *thing-i-ness* of things—the sense of the poet as reliable witness to the world in real time—to say what it was he heard or saw without one extra syllable, to record the moment, the happenstance, the instant when the poet's scrutiny turned its focus to one thing instead of another: *the plums, a red wheelbarrow, the white chickens.* Thus the cinematic, frame-by-frame, lightbeam-of-the-artist's-eye intensity of them, as they made their quite convincing case for Williams's dictum: "No ideas but in things."

Wherefore my nunnish upbringing lent a devotional form, my reading gave a reverential bent to what I saw as the rich internal life and colloquy the poet carries on with language. Poetry, like prayer, might raise language into the face of creation.

"The spiritual life," Bill W. wrote in the text of a fellowship I'm a member of, "is not a theory, we have to live it." The poems here—gathered from books published across three decades—are connected to that spiritual life, their faith claims are in the life of language and its power to make us known to one another and to ourselves.

In the end, my bone rosary is an emblem of what moments of poetry have always meant to me, to wit, a connection where no connection seemed to be, the open beckoning welcome of a new reality, hail and full of grace in which the stuff of creation ceaselessly beats.

ON NEW YEAR'S Eve of 2012, I walked with Seamus Heaney up through Naas, Co. Kildare, behind the corpse of Dennis O'Driscoll to his grave. The late summer of 2013, I rode in the hearse with Heaney's body from Donnybrook in Dublin to Bellaghy in Derry to see him returned to his home ground. Michigan's own Jim Harrison died in March 2016 mid-stanza, slumping over an unfinished poem at his desk in Patagonia. Philip Casey died in Dublin in early 2018, then his countryman and fellow poet Macdara Woods, and two months later Matthew Sweeney—with whom I'd dined once more in Cork—joined this litany of loss.

When Bill died, in April of 2018, I buried him like a pharaoh at the edge of the yard, his elegy cast in bronze, and added his absence to the litany of such sorrowful mysteries that seem to have become the study of my latter years.

On the Feast of All Hallows' Day later that year, I picked up a puppy of the same breed as Bill and named him Carl, after a lost frog my grandsons still grieve.

I live alone on a lake with a dog. That sentence came into my head early in 2020 when I was asked to write a radio script for the BBC that centered on the nature of my quarantine and what it had to do with my writerly life and funerals. I'd been presenting spoken-word pieces on Radio 3 and Radio 4 for twenty-some years and was aware that before language was a written and read thing, language was listened to, a said thing: the lines and sentences we tie together in an effort to measure and test the ideas of things, the things themselves. The pleasure of words in one's mouth, especially when they ring true in both saying and hearing, in both sound and sense, derives from a primal place where language first connects us to others—parents, fellow pilgrims, lovers, gods. Our solitary being becomes community, the solo a colloquy. Language connects us to one another.

Possibly it was this awareness that made me write as if someone might be listening to the words I was placing on the page. Like the bishop's lonesome tree that falls in the forest, a sense that its falling might be perceived, even if only in the spiritual realm. So I was looking for a foot in the door—a first line, an opening moment, a way acoustically into the story I was trying to tell.

Our old dog, long into its dotage, yawns, I remember saying to myself at intervals years ago. My life at the time did not allow sitting to the task of composing a poem. I had a daughter and three sons, toddlers and an infant, a business to run and a wife whose discontents were beginning to shape our lives. There were the double mortgage and utility bills, the credit cards and personal loans. And we had a dog, a Shetland collie named Woolie, adopted before any of the children were born. I was in my early thirties. I was past president of the Rotary Club and of the Chamber of Commerce. I'd published two poems in *Poetry*. I kept a journal in which I wrote every day, in longhand with my grandfather's fountain pen, gifted to me by my grandmother after he died, along with the watch fob and chain his father had given him. I had worn the fob and chain back to Ireland a decade before, before the marriage or the children, the mortgages or the dog, before the decision to go to mortuary school and work with my father in the family business. I brought it back to the stone cottage on the west coast of County Clare it had come out of most of a century before. I was trying, I suppose, to connect the dots, the history and happenstance that had resulted in me. "How do we come to be the ones we are?" is a question I've been long beleaguered by. I've labored over ways to connect the dots between what happened to whom and how it made them who they became.

Our old dog, long into its dotage, yawns seemed a perfect storm of a line: ten syllables, a decade of sound connecting me to so many of my favorite poets and their pentameters, "When you are old and gray and full of sleep," quoth Yeats to his paramour: "What lips my lips have kissed and where, and why," wrote that green-eyed polyamorist Edna St. Vincent Millay. "The thing you fear the most will hunt you down," said the father of a young woman over whose coffined body he stood in the pulpit of the Lutheran church years ago; he wanted to eulogize his dead daughter and set forth on that sad endeavor with "The thing you fear the most will hunt you down." From my seat in the vestibule where I used to listen to these homilies, I found myself tapping out the count of that dark truth: The things we fear the most do hunt us down. I never forgot it.

But what most struck me about *our old dog, long into its dotage, yawns* was not the sense of that moment so much as the sound it made to me, shaped by the open *o*'s—our, old, dog, long, dotage, and the closing *aw* in yawn—which replicated the bodily end to breathing in, to wit, inspiration ends in the spirit entering the body and, thus, expiration, the going out. The open vowels of it became the substance of the sound in pursuit of a further storyline, some sense it was evidently trying to make. It was only a toe in the door of what I hoped would eventually be a poem.

Our old dog, long into its dotage, yawns, I'd say over and over to myself in the middle of any number of endeavors for weeks, for months, and then for years, until one rainy afternoon, on the way back from picking up a body at Henry Ford Hospital on West Grand Boulevard in Detroit, I was northbound on Southfield Road when after saying the line again to myself another decade of syllables attached themselves to that echoing line—"a half-blind version of a breed that bred" and then another, "among the Celts and kept their women clean," in which the rubbing of consonants against their own kind made nice noise where I heard those *b*'s and *c*'s and *cl*'s each of which seemed like a little gift of the language to those of us willing to play in its pool of words and sylla-bles and possible signs.

In the current era, whatever is bad gets worse.

ON MEMORIAL DAY 2020, Americans marked a hundred thou-sand countrymen dead of COVID-19. Names were listed in the *New York Times*. In early July, my long-lost, cruelly afflicted, pre-cious daughter, Heather Grace, whose name I used for my first book of poems, leapt to her death off a bridge in California, bringing the loss of her to its keeps. *Let go*, recovering drunks tell each other, *let God*.

How long will I sit in silence before this mystery?

Black Lives Matter marchers are trying to keep up with the count of bodies of Black men and women shot by police. This long neglected original sin is coming 'round to its reckoning. Never in my life did the sky seem to be falling from all four cor-ners as it seems to now—pandemic, racial injustice, economic collapse, climate change—nor has the body politic, the culture at large, ever seemed so in cahoots as a co-morbidity.

And now it is late summer of 2020. The goldenrod in bloom makes way for the reddening sumac. "How do we come to be the ones we are?" I still ask myself, sitting alone beside the lake with my dog. The bone rosary has lengthened and looped itself, and the installation has been wrapped in blue solar lights that blink like beacons in the dark, signaling the souls of the living and the dead, our cloud of witnesses.

—T.L.
Summer 2020
Mullett Lake, Michigan

The splinters that you carry
The cross you left behind
Come healing of the body
Come healing of the mind

O solitude of longing
Where love has been confined
Come healing of the body
Come healing of the mind

And let the heavens hear it
The penitential hymn
Come healing of the spirit
Come healing of the limb

from "Come Healing,"
Leonard Cohen (1934–2016)

BONE ROSARY

from

SKATING WITH HEATHER GRACE

MICHAEL'S REPLY TO THE WHITE MAN

Listen, mister! I'm not one of those
who feels prenatal in the tub or has some
trauma in his childhood to account
for what it is that dogs me now. I do
no drugs or booze except the sociables
to blow the wondrous coals in me to flame
to where I sing songs, talk in tongues, fix names
to hitherto unknown things. Syllables
are the things I do, and do them carefully
so the great-grandkids of folks like you
will have something from this dire century
besides Freud and wars and hula-hoops.
See, what I'm really after is that tune
God hummed that Monday when he made the world.
What's more, I get paid for it, and pretty good—
unlike my ancient cousin, Mahon "The Crazed."
If you're still after something in my blood,
the blood is his, that wild man's, who raved
up and back the tribal holds of Munster
lamenting the piddling stipend paid to bards,
rhyming in favor of a living wage
for them that lived by rhyming. He was pure outrage.
Which didn't much endear him to his liege lord
who'd no use for those ungrateful hexameters
and might've had poor Mahon's tongue removed,
but it was Ireland, and centuries ago,
and a poet's foibles were pretty much approved
because, though daft, he kept the Histories alive
of kings and cattle raids and their comely wives.
So Mahon was left, more or less, alone.
Which is all I wanted, to be left alone.
And to get some good sleep because I'm bone-

tired of the pace I've had to keep up
day long and all night now for days. See, what
I really need is to get my body and my soul
aligned again with certain kindly stars,
rest and prayer, and after that a few jars
down at McCarthy's and then to hold
my wife in ways that are none of your business.
Actually, mine's a rather fit condition
despite the frenzied notes you're writing down.
I've nothing three weeks in the Knockmealdowns
with the Mrs. wouldn't cure, but Blue Cross is
ill-disposed to pay for that. But mark my words!
I resent your chemicals and diagnoses
and I'm maniac enough to pull a pox
down on the lot of you from the violent ward
upstairs where I have friends—the Halt and Lame
and Cherubim and Seraphim and Archangels.
And I want my belt back, and a change of socks
and a clean shave and my walking papers
with some admission of the mess you've made
in my case and cab fare for the ride home.
Or else I'll do what Mahon would have done.
I'll fire up a baleful Blood Curse poem
to dry the very seed inside you. Once
he wrecked some sniveling Brit who stiffed him
for a wedding song. Old Mahon turned that awful baritone
against the man, who ran off barking or turned to stone.
In all the versions of it, no one missed him.

A DEATH

In the end you want the clean dimensions of it mentioned;
to know the thing adverbially—*while asleep,*
after long illness, tragically in a blaze—

as you would the word of any local weather:
where it gathered, when it got here, how it kept
the traffic at a standstill, slowed the pace,

closed the terminals. Lineage & Issue, Names & Dates—
the facts you gain most confidence in facing—
histories and habitats and whereabouts.

Speak of it, if you speak of it at all, in parts.
The C.V.A. or insufficiency or growth
that grew indifferent to prayer and medication.

Better a tidy science for a heart that stops
than the round and witless horror of someone who
one dry night in perfect humor ceases measurably to be.

VENICE

My wife undressing in the moonlight sleeve by sleeve.
Late duty with our croupy middle son
she got to breathe by coaxing medicine
and VapoRub and steam. She yawns and leaves
the door ajar for closer listening.
Here is how affection settles in. You dream
a girl you had in Venice years ago
off-season, and a room with long windows
so the light she stood in nakedly
danced as the breeze danced in the drapery—
her skin awash in ivory and shadows.
Outside the vaporetti bubble in the water—
Late boats to the Lido and the Zattere.
Down the hall a boy turns in his sleep.

THE BLOOD WE PAID FOR

Our old dog, long into his dotage, yawns—
a half-blind version of a breed that bred
among the Celts and kept their women clean
by barking off the covetous among their kind
when the husbands had gone off pillaging,
making poems and chaos in the next county.

Later, when the Celts themselves had settled in
and took to one god and wearing collars,
their dogs grew tame and even-tempered, tending
sheep and living to a good age; slept for hours
the way our own dog, sprawled on the linoleum,
listens to the breeze sing underneath

the door we never weatherstripped and hears
in some corpuscle of his ancient blood
the rage of wind matting his wet fur back,
sending a lather up from the seawrack
to float among the seabirds, hears them screech
above a band of wild men half-blind with drink,

who, having brought their plunder to the land's end,
ready their flimsy boats along the beach.
It was, of course, the blood we paid for. Spent
good money in bad times for pedigree—
a hundred dollars, fifteen years ago,
for what my wife claimed was a dog with character.

Nor will she let me, much as I'm inclined
(watching the pearlescent cataract
bloom in his good eye) when he's wholly blind,

coax him toward a stand of trees out back
and, because we've both grown overcivilized,
murder him with the utmost dignity.

A FAMILY OF FISHERMEN

In all his dreams of death it was his heart that failed him.
It ran in the family like bellies and tempers
and though his mother's people favored the long pull
and died mostly of kidneys or pneumonias,
skinny and bewildered in their nineties, all
the men drank whiskey and died of big hearts,
huffing and puffing to their purple ends.
So he held to his history and was ever ready
for one bolt out of nowhere that would lay him low
with only the juice left for one last wisdom,
maybe: *I always loved you or I told you so*
or *I must be dreaming.* He must have dreamt
a hundred times of how his great-great-grandfather
after a half day's fishing the cliffs at Doonlickey
could feed the whole parish on pollack and mackerel
till one day somehow he turned up missing
and washed up later in the bay at Goleen
wrapped up in his tackle of ribbons and sinkers
and made, in spite of it, a lovely summer corpse.
So he lit out in the pitch dark with the same instincts,
crossing the winter of his lake to where
he banged at the bare ice till his heart was breaking,
because of beauty, because the cold stars seemed
the blank eyes of women he had always loved,
and he told them so and thought he must be dreaming
to see his family, a family of fishermen,
approaching as the day broke under the snowfall, so
he lay down in the first few inches of it.

TATYANA

Now I've forgotten what you looked like naked.
Dry grief to wonder were the nipples brown,
the breasts so small, or how
the flesh and filigree of bones embraced
in all those postures of your love.
I remember saying once how fine it was
to work a sweat up with you. Then I said
no two get closer than we do at this—
this fretful linkage between bodies.
I made that up of course. I was
frightened and cocksure and might've believed it.
This skin's intelligence, I thought.
Glad tuition of the flesh.
Intimate knowledge of another.
We were, neither of us, certain.
Now we are old friends. We meet for drinks.
The talk is cautious and well-read,
affecting ignorance and equilibrium.
Sometimes I think I can see you laid bare again.
I think I see you naked when your eyes
turn aimlessly beyond our conversation
into the air where we make our visit and where
nothing ever happens. Nothing has.

LIKE MY FATHER WAKING EARLY

Even for an undertaker, it was odd.
My father always listened through the dark,
half-dreaming hours to a radio
that only played police and fire tunes.
Mornings, he was all the news of break-ins, hold-ups,
now and then a house gone up in flames
or a class of disorder he'd call, frowning,
a *Domestic*. They were dying in our sleep.
My father would sit with his coffee and disasters,
smoking his Luckies, reading the obits.
"I've buried boys who played with matches
or swam alone or chased balls into the streets
or ate the candy that a stranger gave them. . ."
or so he told us as a form of caution.
When I grew older, the boys he buried toyed
with guns or drugs or drink or drove too fast
or ran with the wrong crowd headlong into peril.
One poor client hanged himself from a basement rafter—
heartsick, as my father told it, for a girl.
By sixteen, I assisted with bodies,
preparing them for burial in ways
that kept my dread of what had happened to them busy
with arteries and veins and chemistries—
a safe and scientific cousin, once removed
from the horror of movements they never made.
Nowadays I bury children on my own.
Last week two six-year-olds went through the ice
and bobbed up downstream where the river bends
through gravel and shallows too fast to freeze.
We have crib deaths and cancers, suicides,
deaths in fires, deaths in cars run into trees,
and now I understand my father better.

I've seen the size of graves the sexton digs
to bury futures in, to bury children.
Upstairs, my children thrive inside their sleep.
Downstairs, I'm tuning in the radio.
I do this like my father, waking early,
I have my coffee, cigarettes and worry.

MARRIAGE

He wanted a dry mouth, whiskey and warm flesh
and for all his bothersome senses to be still.
He let his eyeballs roll back in their sockets until
there was only darkness. He grew unmindful
of the spray of moonwash that hung in the curtains,
the dry breath of the furnace, parts of a tune
he'd hummed to himself all day. Any noise
that kept him from his own voice hushed.
He wanted to approximate the effort of snowdrift,
to gain that sweet position over her repose
that always signaled to her he meant business,
that turned them into endless lapping dunes.
He wanted her mouth to fill like a bowl of vowels,
prime and whole and invisible, O. . .O. . .O. . .

LESSONS FROM BERKELEY

Dualco, Dualco. . .Why do we bother
to figure and refigure these old formulae?
What can it matter if
knowing these grand axioms binds us no less?
The Laws of Life: We breathe
or blink, say, twenty times a minute.
Twice in a good month we have dreams
of sweet delirium. Once
every ten years, more or less,
a heartbreak or some big luck in the lottery.
One birth, one death, a marriage and a half, one
in between. Between the two of us
my brains are sore from it.
Let God keep watch tonight and listen for
the tree falling in the forest,
all that well-kept- secret, human noise
of new birth, lovers, and nearly dead,
any distant smack or boom or bleat
by hearing which He earns His endless keep.
Esse est percipere, Dualco—
To be etc., etc.
Let's you and me go out and drink to excess as
if it were required of our kind
to blight our senses now and then, get blind
and willing and benign,
like particles of some vast perception:
the rock and wave and all unfeeling things
that outlive by a longshot
things that think or see or sense,
articles of their own impermanence.

O CANADA

Some nights he'd watch hockey and so she'd rock
with a novel or her Valéry and go to France
where she and several guests of the gay prince
picnic and play at croquet on the château grounds.
Lace and ribbons are all the fashion rage
and ladies in chiffon and high coiffures
fan their bright bosoms like birds of song.
And there are men with names like pink flowers
or instruments of sound in silk stockings
and plump satin breeches to knee length who seem fond
of dabbing their rouged lips with handkerchiefs
they keep in their coat sleeves for such occasions
while all around their wigs hum yellow honeybees,
drawn to their powders and colognes and toiletries.
And she is out among them. And her hand is kissed
by gentlemen of rank and her opinion sought
on Couperin and Molière and Poussin—
all high etiquette and courtly talk.
Out in the garden, she hears the gardener sing,
between hedgerows of juniper and yew,
O Canada, our home and native land. He moves
by evening light through his green diocese,
smelling of dung and mulch and growing things,
heartsick for that hard country of his youth.
Some nights he'd take her to his room upstairs
and speak in that far dialect she loved
of ice and earth qualities of air—
his True North, strong and free, O Canada;
and then he'd make hardbody love to her.
Next morning she'd make omelettes and he'd thumb
the newspaper for word if Guy Lafleur
or Marcel Dionne. And she'd be pleased because
that was the style of the country he'd come from.

THE WIDOW

Her life was spent in deference to his comfort.
The rocking chair was his, the window seat,
the firm side of the mattress.

Hers were the midnights with sickly children,
pickups after guests left, the single
misery of childbirth. She had duties:

to feed him and to follow and to forgive his few
excesses. Sometimes he drank, he puffed cigars,
he belched, he brought the money in

and brought Belleek and Waterford for birthdays,
rings and rare scents for Christmas; twice he sent
a card with flowers: "All my love, always."

At night she spread herself like linen out
for him to take feastly pleasures in
and liked it well enough, or said she did, day in,

day out. For thirty years they agreed on this
until one night, after dinner dancing,
he died a gassy death at fifty—turned

a quiet purple in his chair, quit breathing.
She grieved for him with a real grief for she missed him
sorely. After six months of this, she felt relieved.

A DREAM OF DEATH IN THE FIRST PERSON

I'm coming the coast road into Moveen.
This part replays itself, over and over
to a standstill, until I'm hardly moving.
Out in the ocean are islands I've never
noticed in pictures I have of that place.
I take this as a signal I'm dreaming.
Within the dream, then, I begin to bless
myself against such peril as these dreams
in all their early versions put me in.
In one, great soaring gulls keep coaxing me,
by angles of their flight I understand,
to join them in the air beyond the land
and make my life with them diving between islands.

SKATING WITH HEATHER GRACE

Apart from the apparent values,
there are lessons in circular:
paradigms for history,
time in a round world, turning,
love with another of your species—

To watch my only daughter
widening her circles is to ease
headlong into the traffic
of her upbringing.

Until nearly four she screamed
at my absence, mourned
my going out for any reason,
cried at scoldings,
agreed to common lies regarding
thunder, Christmas,
baby teeth. Last year

she started school
without incident;
this year ballet and new math. Soon

I think my love will seem
entirely deficient.

Later there's the hokey-pokey
and dim lights for the partners' dance.
She finds a shaky nine-year-old
to skate around
in counterclockwise orbits,
laughing.

Is it more willingness than balance?
Is letting go the thing that keeps her steady?

I lean against the sideboards sipping
coffee. I keep a smile ready.

LEARNING GRAVITY

Here is how it happens. One soft night
you're sitting in an outdoor bar with friends,
glad for the long days and your own survival,
which has come for the time being to depend
upon what conversation you can make
out of Beethoven or the cinema,
out of the way the loss of light proceeds
from top to bottom in the sky, always
abiding by those few sure-footed laws
whereby things rise and fall, arrive and take
their leave according to their gravity—
earthbound, in balance, timely and at ease.
When who shows up among the tabletops
but somebody you haven't seen in years.
You follow him into another room
and find him staring in a wall of mirrors.
He doesn't know how long it's been or what
he's done. He has no plans, he says, except
to be gone tomorrow. Much later, on
account of this, you will begin to grieve.

That time in Moveen, the sky became
so full of motion the soft air seemed
too quick a think to breathe in, so I sang

out where the gulls glide on the edge of weather
songs in praise of rootlessness and wayfare
and wore my newfound whereabouts with honor

the way a man does who goes traveling
without a war on or a famine:
c/o third cousins, West Clare, Ireland.

My Love, I wrote home in a letter, here
the old arrangement of the rock & water
gathers up the coastline in a lather.

The slate cliffs lean with the weight of the land
into the heft & heave of ocean.
I watch the tide fall and rise and fall again.

I thought of you then as a secret in the water
that made waves out of the elements of order
and taught them surge and swell and billow

so the air filled with rich noise below
the tall ledge of land I edged along
dizzy with the sweet enticement of the fall.

Kennedy had been dead by then for years.
My fall from innocence
began with a still frame from Zapruder's film—
a blurry likeness of the way he leaned
into his wife's hug with the look of damage,
and how she cuddled him as if he were
a bingy drunk who only liquored up
for holidays or funerals or for fun.
I thought, how much she loves him,
how surely dead he seems. Since then
I measure my departure from where I was
that day, in Christian Brothers' School
and the flat voice on the PA saying
all that we could do was pray.
I put you with the nuns, next door, that day—
your life in those times parallel with mine,
arranged by height or alphabet for sacraments.
First Communion, Confirmation,
the Death of Presidents.

I remember my poor cousin in his bed.
A quiet replica of calm,
his mouth propped shut with his daily missal.
A rosary kept his hands crossed on his chest.
Inside the women hummed their beads and sipped
sweet wine and ripe Cidona. In the yard
the men complained of prices and the spring that left
a mudwreck of their fields and kept their cows in.
"The Lord've mercy on him, Tommy was
a daycent man he was and innocent.
A pure St. Francis with his cattle, shy
when it came to women or the drink.
Sure Faith, there was no speck of sin in him."
And then in deference to his Yankee namesake,
bloodshot from the porter or the grief,
they brought their hopeless talk around to Kennedy.

His was the first death in our lives that took.
Until then our heroes were invincible:
the cartoon cat who swallows dynamite,
the cowpoke who turns up in a rodeo
after getting murdered in a bar fight.
That was the apple we bit for truth:
the permanence of death for him, for us
the death of permanence. For days
we watched him go the way of the
Friday Meat Rule and the Latin Mass,
the rhythm method, black-and-white TV,
true love and romance, our favorite saints,
Cardinal Sins, Contrary Virtues, all
parts of life we'd made a part of us that changed.
O Jack, here twenty years since then
we only think of you as dead.

Your pink notes came up the coast road with the postman.
Word about friends, weddings, and the spring

in Michigan, and Roethke, whose growth of poems
you'd grown enamored of. "He sings and sings

root tunes and seed songs, hums the fern and foliage."
Of course, he'd learned the lesson in his garden—

how one day getting on to autumn
you come across hard knowledge like a corpse

left out in the dull light by some passion,
murderous or accidental, nonetheless

passion of a human sort. You appraise the body's beauty:
a leptosome among the leaves. The rare lines

of the ribs poke out beneath the skin
like kite-work of some former elegance. The leaves rise on

the small ground wind. The birdlike beauty lies
solid in its lack of movement, quiet as the moon is,

drinking the darkness like the moon does, turning
damp and fertile. Going to seed.

With this intelligence you begin, then,
thick with excitement and new fright.

I remember the bones of my kinsmen,
long since dead, unearthed again in the graves'
reopening—femurs and half-skulls and ribs

in piles at graveside at Moyarta.
And the general reverence of townsmen,
neighbors, thick countrymen from the creamery
or local bog, thatchers and fishermen,
all of whom had doings with our newly dead.
All of whom had come to their consensus
after mass in boozy In Memoriams:
"An honest airy man he was. By cripes,
the saint of the peninsula! A far,
far better specimen than the likes of us."
When the priest said so, we made for Moyarta,
shouldering the saint of that peninsula
into the hilly middle ground between
the River Shannon's mouth and the North Atlantic.

Consider Roethke in his tub at Mercywood,
crazy with his glad mayhem, how he would
soak for hours like a length of bogwood

lolling and bobbing in the water.
I think of you, your body in the water
and how the light glistened in the beads of water

that ran down between your breasts like islands
among the bare geographies I learned
the year that we were lovers, after Ireland.

Who knows how all things alter in the seed?
From shoot to stem to full bloom, then to seed,
clumsy with their own invention until they see

that everything that breathes requires death.
A fierce affection is a thing like death.
Love begets love, then life, then death.

I watch the river wind itself away,
delighted at your bright flesh drying, at the way
the earthly body learns its earthly ways.

1948—Expect from birth
68.6 years, give or take.
A useful figure for, say, figuring
career options, life goals, middle age,
with further applications in the abstract:
to arrive at what to expect from death, subtract
the Useful Figure from Infinity.
The Crude Death Rate for 1963 was
nine point four per thousand, which includes
infant mortality, less the fetal deaths,
a poet, Roethke, and a President.
1970—some notable variants:
bad flu in the Middle West,
the same war in Asia, always
pestilence in the usual places.
The remarkable number: 100%.

I'm the one who keeps a rough count of the dead.
I count whatever's unclaimed after months
of reasonable inquiries, want ads, word of mouth—
things get around once word gets out.
It's a small place we live in, after all.
Which explains the recent interest in your case.
Because it seems you've come into your strength
so that you fall no faster than thirty-two
feet per second per second and you move
always in accordance with the rules of life
that govern bodies moving in the realm of light.
What is it you keep faith in, hope for,

count your blessings by? Life after death?
Death after life? After sex a cigarette?
Why is it I have come to think of you without
a history or vision or the dreadful tow
of things that moved us and the way we went
out into the real world full of innocence,
passion, and mortality? I don't know.
But things happen every day here.
We could all be alive tomorrow.

Sometimes I come here for a drink with friends.
Sometimes I drink too much and feel like crying
God, God! I'm a sad man with a thin heart dying
from complications of a complex race of men
who all their lives look for holes to fill
with all their lives. Their lives and loss of will.

A CLEARING IN THE WOODS

You have come into a clearing in the woods
and want to live your life out, here, alone,
joyous and remote among the catbirds

letting the light fall on you and the shade
in hourly changing angles as a grace
endlessly descending among tree limbs

while growing in you is the will to grow
mindless of the niggling everyday
profusion of detail by which you know

uselessly the names and dates and shapes of things.
After a while, you will begin to sing.
Harmless and plentiful you make the sounds.

Bent on nothing that does not bend with ease
you and your song rise in the leafy air
chancy as bass spawn in a mallard's underwings.

A NOTE ON THE RAPTURE TO HIS TRUE LOVE

A blue bowl on the table in the dining room
fills with sunlight. From a sunlit room
I watch my neighbor's sugar maple turn
to shades of gold. It's late September. Soon. . .
Soon as I'm able I intend to turn
to gold myself. Somewhere I've read that soon
they'll have a formula for prime numbers
and once they do, the world's supposed to end
the way my neighbor always said it would—
in fire. I'll bet we'll all be given numbers
divisible by One and by themselves
and told to stand in line the way you would
for prime cuts at the butcher's. In the end,
maybe it's every man for himself.
Maybe it's someone hollering All Hands on
Deck! Abandon Ship! Women and Children First!
Anyway, I'd like to get my hands on
you. I'd like to kiss your eyelids and make love
as if it were our last time, or the first,
or else the one and only form of love
divisible by which I yet remain myself.
Mary, folks are disappearing one by one.
They turn to gold and vanish like the leaves
of sugar maples. But we can save ourselves.
We'll pick our own salvations, one by one,
from a blue bowl full of sunlight until none is left.

PORNOGRAPHY

My father had a *Bell's Pathology*.
He studied it in Mortuary School.
A thick pictorial of sicknesses
so grisly or disfiguring or rare.
There was a man whose one leg never grew,
in boxer shorts, a giant held a she-dwarf,
Siamese twins joined at the belly,
a hapless lady with a goiter
and foreign names for each my father englished as:
"As kids they hardly touched their vegetables."

Pat's dad kept a stack of magazines
hidden under stairs down to the basement.
Inside them, breathless shapes stretched out in satin—
like figurines in porcelain at rest,
and held their breath so that their breasts swelled
like rare new forms of intelligent life
and held our broad arousal with the way
a bent knee, a bit of lingerie,
or the edge of light itself, in those days,
hid from Pat and me their most illegal parts.

THE LITURGIST

Pressing the linens for Thanksgiving, she
recalls the bright dress she married in—
tight lace and organdy; how after ironing
she held it to herself, arm over arm,
like a thin partner in a dance and danced
in slow approving turns around the room
like the morning of her first communion:
ready as she'd been for anything, ever—
for the first time with him, the mix of sweat
and sweet breath, fond percussion, how she pressed
beneath the low commotion of their lovemaking.
It seemed to her then like the care of linens
or the care of children, or in spring,
like pressing new seeds into her garden
or the meal she spreads out for Thanksgiving:
a portion chore, a portion sacrament.

I FELT MYSELF TURNING

I felt myself turning, circling downward,
The shape of my descent put me in mind
of Yeats or tornadoes or the way seabirds,
focusing their hunger over baitfish shoals,
would fall in tightening spirals off the wind.
I kept trying to formulate a set of goals
or a plan on the off-chance it all would end
with my being offered one final chance
to make good, a last meal, or a cigarette.
There was a comfort in those great gulls, how they bent
against their fatal gravity—at the last
moment turning up with fish, effortless
in their ascension, full of hope, they seemed
a new life-form light-years removed from me.

A GOOD DEATH EVEN WHEN IT KILLS YOU

Afterwards, she watched the snowfall closely,
counting her blessings from a window indoors,
where only the low din of tableware
and hushed neighbors among the casseroles
trespassed her focus on the ghost-white weather.
Anyway, he was doing what he liked most—
out before daylight with his shanty and lanterns,
wax-worms and jig poles, thermos and brandy;
the whole lashup in long tow on foot to where
last night his calculations put a school of bluegill—
instead of hooked to some intensive hardware
to chart and graph and lengthen the whole thing,
or long suffering to the same end with a cancer
or half a dozen other ways she knew of. No,
this was a quick and lethal one, according
to the coroner. And she was glad for him.
A good death, even when it kills you, is
nonetheless some better than a bad one.
When the snow quit falling, there was still the lake
and then a stubble of cornfield uphill in rows
and then two birds above a stand of winter oaks
circling in the gray unfocused space of weather.
When she could see no farther, she began to hate him
for fifteen years of rearing children and
for cold nights when she warmed against him and for
all the tender habits he observed in love, because
he was all she'd ever wanted and was dead at forty,
spudding the ice for a hole, to get a line in.

TO HER SISTERS ON THE NATURE
OF THE UNIVERSE

I think of all landscapes as feminine
and of the many seasons as a man
whose weather is the ever-changing reason
he will give for wanting you. As for hands,
I think of them as daybreak and nightfall
hourly easing over my skin. My skin
is the morning you awaken to snowfall
drifting to berms and swells and shallowings
like tidal oceans overtaking land.
I think of oceans as the way a man
returns to me from exile or wars,
blood-drunk and frightened to the bone. Of course
he hears her then, asleep between my breasts—
the angel charged with beckoning the dead;
and wakes up gladsome for the soft iambic code
my pulse assures him with: Not yet, not yet.

WHERE IT CAME FROM

Where it came from if it came from anywhere
was the deep pit within him where his anger was
hunched like a bad beast back on its haunches
ready to hunker up whenever he got ready
whenever he'd had enough of this or when
love turned sour left him out of love.

Trouble was whenever he got troubled
by something lesser men got lessened by
or needled by some needless hurt or
thought of some lost intimate he only thought
Good God! Might all this come to some last good
to ease the ache I've grown lately accustomed to?

Furthermore he seemed to draw no further
comfort from those things he once drew comfort
from: Ease of wit and easy motion from
one good hideout to another. Once
when he was at his peak of loneliness he went
nowhere for a good long while where he wasn't known.

NOON ON SATURDAY

I.

The fire whistle sets the dogs to howling,
adding their odd song to the sound of damage,
and everywhere folks seem to carry on
like nothing has happened. And nothing has.
No emergency. It's noon on Saturday.
Most Saturdays at noon I sit like this,
a thankless member of my subspecies,
at odds with all the elements of grace—
the wife and kids, the furnace kicking on—
able to manage only this much faith:
Life goes on. I say this to myself. Life goes on.
I rummage in the house for signs of loss.

II.

I watch winter out the window gathering.
White where the ground was, gray where the sky was,
a company of blackbirds in a walnut tree
holding forth, no doubt, about the weather:
The winter, you say, will be long and cold.
The frost will deepen in the earth, the light
grow shorter till there seems no light at all.
O to have the bird's life in the air, to roll
on the air above the worst weather,
to say I saw the whole thing from the sky—
the way the cold comes this time most years,
the same way as the darkness, and our flight.

III.

Same as the way I'm inclined to sit here
hour after hour because my life
seems oddly affected by the weather,
by the sight of cold birds in a bald tree
grieving the winter, figuring a way out.
When all I ever needed for a little warmth
was to pay the gas man and the ones I love
or to sing the same song over and over
because the sound it makes keeps me intact
like the one long note that signals danger,
proclaims a fire or a cardiac
out in the township or noon on Saturday.

WORMWOOD

The one who took a pistol in his teeth
and blew his brains across the family room
and how his wife, for weeks, found little pieces
of his skull wedged in the wormwood paneling
as tokens of his longstanding discontent
provides a body for my deadly sentiment.
Or what about the one who lay between
his Buick's dual exhausts and breathed and breathed
until he was out of breath and at a loss
to say exactly what it was that went wrong.
There were, of course, the usual theories.

PRUNING

She wonders do they feel
the loss of limbs as we do,
bristling in the air like haloes
over picture saints,
the prickly heat beyond
the stump's thick suturing,
the phantom hollering downstairs
for towels or clean socks,
shampoo or shaving cream.
Last year he did the
lilac and mock orange himself,
in June. He stood in the kitchen
sun-brown and penitent and said
an early cutting makes
somehow for better blooms.
At night she holds his pillow
to her ribs and rubs
carefully the rough edge of her wound.

THE GRANDMOTHERS

A hundred sixty years of lucid memory sit
under a plump umbrella on the patio—
two widows nursing whiskey sours argue politics:

my grandmothers. When they turned eighty, we began
to mark their changes as we might a child's
in terms of sight, mobility and appetite,

teeth and toilet habits, clarity of speech,
a thousand calibers of round flight
by which my children make their distance now from me.

Sometimes I think of them as parts of me.
I think their ageless quarrels come to roost
like odd birds with an awkward plumage in my blood.

The one says tend your own twigs, peep and preen.
The other wings beyond the kindly orbit here
and sings, and sings, and sings.

FOR THE EX-WIFE ON THE OCCASION
OF HER BIRTHDAY

Let me say outright that I bear you no
unusual malice anymore. Nor
do I wish for you tumors or loose stools,
blood in your urine, oozings from any orifice.
The list is endless of those ills I do not pray befall you:
night sweats, occasional itching, PMS,
fits, starts, ticks, boils, bad vibes, vaginal odors,
emotional upheavals or hormonal disorders;
green discharge, lumps, growths, nor tell-tale signs of gray;
dry heaves, hiccups, heartbreaks, fallen ovaries
nor cramps—before, during, or after. I pray you only
laughter in the face of your mortality
and freedom from the ravages of middle age:
bummers, boredom, cellulite, toxic shock and pregnancies;
migraines, glandular problems, the growth of facial hair,
sagging breasts, bladder infections, menopausal rage,
flatulence or overdoses, hot flashes or constant nausea,
uterine collapse or loss of life or limb or faith
in the face of what might seem considerable debilities.
Think of your life not as half-spent but as half-full
of possibilities. The Arts maybe, or
Music, Modern Dance, or Hard Rock Videos.
Whatever, this is to say I hereby recant
all former bitterness and proffer only all the best
in the way of Happy Birthday wishes.
I no longer want your mother committed,
your friends banished, your donkey lovers taken out and shot
or spayed or dragged behind some Chevrolet of doom.
I pray you find that space or room or whatever it is
you and your shrink have always claimed you'd need
to spread your wings and realize your insuperable potential.

Godspeed is what I say, and good credentials:
what with your background in fashion and aerobics,
you'd make a fairly bouncy brain surgeon
or well-dressed astronaut or disc jockey.
The children and I will be watching with interest
and wouldn't mind a note from time to time
to say you've overcome all obstacles this time;
overcome your own half-hearted upbringing,
a skimpy wardrobe, your lowly self-esteem,
the oppression of women and dismal horoscopes;
overcome an overly dependent personality,
stretch marks, self-doubt, a bad appendix scar,
the best years of your life misspent on wifing and mothering.
So let us know exactly how you are once
you have triumphed, after all. Poised and ready
on the brink of, shall we say, your middle years,
send word when you have gained by the luck of the draw,
the kindness of strangers, or the dint of will itself
if not great fame then self-sufficiency.
Really, now that I've my hard-won riddance of you
signed and sealed and cooling on the books against
your banks and creditors; now that I no
longer need endure your whining discontent,
your daylong, nightlong, carping over lost youth,
bum luck, spilt milk, what you might have been,
or pining not so quietly for a new life in
New York with new men; now that I have been
more or less officially relieved of
all those hapless duties husbanding
a woman of your disenchantments came to be,
I bid you No Deposits, No Returns,
but otherwise a very Happy Birthday.
And while this mayn't sound exactly like good will
in some important ways it could be worse.

The ancients in my family had a way with words
and overzealous habits of revenge
whereby the likes of you were turned to birds
and made to nest among the mounds of dung
that rose up in the wake of cattle herds
grazing their way across those bygone parishes
where all that ever came with age was wisdom.

from

GRIMALKIN & OTHER POEMS

ATTENDE DOMINE

To lie in the tub on New Year's morning
awash in bath oil and resolution,
observing the Feast of the Circumcision,
is to seek the water's absolution
according to the law that juxtaposes
Cleanliness and Godliness. I suppose
it is time to examine my conscience,
to make a clean breast of it and amends
to such as those I might have offended.
Attende Domine et miserere! Lord
I've sinned with my eye and did not pluck it out,
and with my hand and yet my hand remains
blessing myself against Your righteousness.
I've sinned with my mouth and loved the sound it made.

AISLING

Whenever he left her
there was always a landscape
into which he would bring her
in her linen dress
to circle a fir tree
where blackbirds were nesting
in the first green field
beyond the formal gardens.
He would sit at the big desk
in the bay window
in the west room they'd given him
to do it in.
He would try to describe it—
the shape of her turning
and the tune she was humming
and the way she drew
the hem of her dress up
with her small arms rising
and falling and rising
in a kind of flight.
He would try to decide if
later, by evening,
when the light was behind her
if she really knew
how the lines of her body
sharpened by twilight
would step from her clothing
in a silhouette,
if she knew how it filled him
with grief and desire
watching the gardens
and the green go black

while birds in the fir tree
settled into silence
and the great bay window
darkened where he sat—
a dark so black
he could never, ever
let her into it.

AT THE OPENING OF OAK GROVE
CEMETERY BRIDGE

Before this bridge we took the long way around
up First Street to Commerce, then left at Main,
taking our black processions down through town
among storefronts declaring *Dollar Days!*
Going Out of Business! Final Mark Downs!
Then pausing for the light at Liberty,
we'd make for the Southside by the Main Street bridge
past used car sales and party stores as if
the dead required one last shopping spree
to finish their unfinished business.
Then eastbound on Oakland by the jelly-works,
the landfill site, and unmarked railroad tracks—
by bump and grinding motorcade we'd come
to bury our dead by the river at Oak Grove.

And it is not so much that shoppers gawked
or merchants carried on irreverently,
as many bowed their heads or paused or crossed
themselves against their own mortalities.
It's that bereavement is a cottage industry,
a private enterprise that takes in trade
long years of loving for long years of grief.
The heart cuts bargains in a marketplace
that opens afterhours when the stores are dark
and Christmases and Sundays when the hard
currencies of void and absences
nickel and dime us into nights awake
with soured appetites and shaken faith
and a numb hush fallen on the premises.

Such stillness leaves us moving room by room
rummaging through the cupboards and the closetspace
for any remembrance of our dead lovers,
numbering our losses by the noise they made
at home—in basements tinkering with tools
or in steamy bathrooms where they sang in the shower,
in kitchens where they labored over stoves
or gossiped over coffee with the next-door neighbor,
in bedrooms where they made their tender moves;
whenever we miss that division of labor
whereby he washes, she dries; she dreams, he snores;
he does the storm window, she does floors;
she nods in the rocker, he dozes on the couch;
he hammers a thumbnail, she says Ouch!

This bridge allows a residential route.
So now we take our dead by tidy homes
with fresh bedlinens hung in the backyards
and lanky boys in driveways shooting hoops
and gardens to turn and lawns for mowing
and young girls sunning in their bright new bodies.
First to Atlantic and down Mont-Eagle
to the marshy north bank of the Huron
where blue heron nest, rock-bass and bluegill
bed in the shallows and life goes on.
And on the other side, the granite rows
of Johnsons, Jacksons, Ruggles, Wilsons, Smiths—
the common names we have in common with
this place, this river and these winter-oaks.

And have, likewise in common, our own ends
that bristle in us when we cross this bridge—
the cancer or the cardiac arrest

or lapse of caution that will do us in.
Among these stones we find the binding thread:
old wars, old famines, whole families killed by flus,
a century and then some of our dead
this bridge restores our easy access to.
A river is a decent distance kept.
A graveyard is an old agreement made
between the living and the living who have died
that says we keep their names and dates alive.
This bridge connects our daily lives to them
and makes them, once our neighbors, neighbors once again.

GREEN BANANAS

My father quit buying
green bananas
for what he said were the
obvious reasons.
And made no plans—the seasons
giving way to days or parts of days
spent waiting for the deadly embolus
the doctors always talked about
to lodge
itself sideways
in some important spot
between his last breath and the one
that would not be coming after that.
Then he said Let's
go out for Chinese.
He had won-ton soup, eggrolls,
sweet and sour,
grinned when he opened the fortune
cookie. Winked at the waitress.
Left her a huge tip.
Was dead inside a month.

ADORO TE DEVOTE

Father Kenny taught me Latin hymns.
And, lost for words, I'd often chant Gregorian:
Adoro te devote, latens Deitas—
a second tongue, more humbly to adore them in,
those hidden dieties: the bodies of women,
the bodies of men, their sufferings and passions,
the sacred mysteries of life and death
by which our sight and touch and taste are all deceived.
By hearing only safely we believe.
And so I listened and am still listening.
I've heard the prayers said over open graves
and heard the pleas of birth and lovemaking.
O God! O God! we always seem to say.
And God, God help us, answers Wait and see.

GRIMALKIN

One of these days she will lie there and be dead.
I'll take her out back in a garbage bag
and bury her among my sons' canaries,
the ill-fated turtles, a pair of angelfish:
the tragic and mannerly household pests
that had the better sense to take their leaves
before their welcomes or my patience had worn thin.
For twelve long years I've suffered this damned cat
while Mike, my darling middle-son, himself
twelve years this coming May, has grown into
the tender if quick-tempered man-child
his breeding blessed and cursed him to become.
And only his affection keeps this cat alive
though more than once I've threatened violence—
the brick and burlap in the river recompense
for mounds of furballs littering the house,
choking the vacuum cleaner, or what's worse:
shit in the closets, piss in the planters, mice
that winter indoors safely as she sleeps
curled about a table-leg, vigilant
as any knickknack in a partial coma.
But Mike, of course, is blind to all of it—
the gray Angora breed of arrogance,
the sluttish roar, the way she disappears for days
sex-desperate once or twice a year,
urgently ripping her way out the screen door
to have her way with anything that moves
while Mike sits up with tuna fish and worry,
crying into the darkness "here kitty kitty,"
mindless of her whorish treacheries;
or of her crimes against upholsteries—
the sofas, love seats, wingbacks, easy chairs

she's puked and mauled into dilapidation.
I have this recurring dream of driving her
deep into the desert east of town
and dumping her out there with a few days' feed
and water. In the dream, she's always found
by kindly tribespeople who eat her kind
on certain holy days as a form of penance.
God knows, I don't know what he sees in her.
Sometimes he holds her like a child in his arms
rubbing her underside until she sounds
like one of those battery-powered vibrators
folks claim to use for the ache in their shoulders.
And under Mike's protection she will fix her
indolent green-eyed gaze on me as if
to say: Whaddaya gonna do about it, Slick,
the child loves me and you love the child.
Truth told, I really ought to have her fixed
in the old way with an airtight alibi,
a bag of ready-mix and no eyewitnesses.
But one of these days she will lie there and be dead.
And choking back loud hallelujahs, I'll pretend
a brief bereavement for my Michael's sake,
letting him think as he has often said
"deep down inside you really love her don't you Dad."
I'll even hold some cheerful obsequies
careful to observe God's never-failing care
for even these, the least of His creatures,
making some mention of cat-heaven where
cat-ashes to ashes, cat-dust to dust
and the Lord gives and the Lord has taken away.
Thus claiming my innocence to the end,
I'll turn Mike homeward from that wicked little grave
and if he asks, we'll get another one because
all boys need practice in the arts of love
and all boys' aging fathers in the arts of rage.

CASABLANCA

It is always an airport
or a railway station
or one of those airy dockside rooms
folks wait in watching for the boats that move
on schedule between the outer islands.
I'm home from the big war
or a concert tour.
The news is full of my vast heroics.
One of my entourage has gone for the limo.
Another is waiting at the baggage claim.
I'm considering titles for the movie version.
And there you are, there you are, again.
Having finished your work here you have come to book
your passage on the next departure.
You are more beautiful than ever.
All of the men who loved you are dead or vanished.
I am the last man on the face of the century.

IN PARADISUM

Sometimes I look into the eyes of corpses.
They are like mirrors broken, frozen pools,
or empty tabernacles, doors left open,
vacant and agape; like votives cooling,
motionless as stone in their cold focus.
As if they'd seen something. As if it all
came clear to them, at long last, in that last moment
of light perpetual or else the black
abyss of requiems and nothingness.
Only the dead know what the vision is,
beholding which they wholly faint away
amid their plenary indulgences.
In Paradisum, deducante we pray:
their first sight of what is or what isn't.

INVIOLATA

I had a nunnish upbringing. I served
six-twenty Mass on weekdays for a priest
who taught me the *Confetior* and to keep
a running tally of the things I'd done
against the little voice in me the nuns
were always saying I should listen to.
And listen is what I did and spoke the truth
of it to Father Kenny in confession,
and walked out with a clean slate, listening,
listening. At thirteen what it said was Tits.
Tits everywhere. Even Sr. Jean Térèse—
Inviolata, integra et casta—
for all her blue habits and scapular,
standing at the blackboard, sideways, couldn't hide them.

LIBERTY

Some nights I go out and piss on the front lawn
as a form of freedom—liberty from
porcelain and plumbing and the Great Beyond
beyond the toilet and the sewage works.
Here is the statement I am trying to make:
to say I am from a fierce bloodline of men
who made their water in the old way, under stars
that overarched the North Atlantic where
the River Shannon empties into sea.
The ex-wife used to say, Why can't you pee
in concert with most of humankind
who do their business tidily indoors?
It was gentility or envy, I suppose,
because I could do it anywhere, and do
whenever I begin to feel encumbered.
Still, there is nothing, here in the suburbs,
as dense as the darkness in West Clare
nor any equivalent to the nightlong wind
that rattles in the hedgerow of whitethorn there
on the east side of the cottage yard in Moveen.
It was market day in Kilrush, years ago:
my great-great-grandfather bargained with tinkers
who claimed it was whitethorn that Christ's crown was made from.
So he gave them two and six and brought them home—
mere saplings then—as a gift for the missus,
who planted them between the house and garden.
For years now, men have slipped out the back door
during wakes or wedding feasts or nights of song
to pay their homage to the holy trees
and, looking up into that vast firmament,
consider liberty in that last townland where
they have no crowns, no crappers, and no ex-wives.

NO PRISONERS

Odds are the poor man was trying to please her
because her pleasure would have pleasured him,
adding as it would have to his image of
himself as a latter-day Man of Steel,
able as always to leap tall buildings
and off whose chest the bullets would bounce,
his five bypasses notwithstanding,
nor withstanding how his heart had grown
flimsy with hard loving and bereavement.
Or maybe it was the Marine Lance-Corporal
in the snapshot of himself in the South Pacific
he kept in the corner of the bathroom mirror:
bare-chested in khakis and boondockers
with Billy Swinford Smith from Paris, Kentucky,
posing as always for the girls back home;
the ready and willing eighteen-year-old
who went from right tackle with St. Francis DeSalles
to light machine-gunner with the Corps
and came home skinny and malarial later
to marry the redheaded girl of his dreams
who had written him daily through the war,
beginning her letters with *My Darling Edward*
and closing with *All My Love Always, Rose.*
We found those letters, years later, in a drawer
and tried to imagine them both young again,
dancing to Dorsey and Glenn Miller tunes
under the stars at the Walled Lake Pavilion
before they had any idea of us.
"Six sons," he'd laugh, "enough for Pallbearers!
And girls enough to keep us in old age."
So when our mother took to her bed with cancer,
it was, of course, the girls who tended her

while my brothers and I sat with him downstairs,
being brave for each other. When she died
he knelt by her bedside sobbing "Rosie,
my darling, what will I do without you?"
And grieved his grief like Joe DiMaggio
who never missed a game and took a rose
to place in the vase at her graveside daily,
then came home to sit in his chair and weep,
those first nights without her thereby replacing
as the worst in his life a night in '44
on Walt's Ridge in Cape Gloucester, New Britain,
when he and elements of the First Marines
survived nine Bonzai charges. The Japanese
foot-soldiers kept screaming, kept coming, blind
into the crossfire of light machine guns
that he and Billy and Donald Crescent Coe
kept up all night aiming just below the voices.
In the morning he crawled out of his hole
to poke his bayonet among the dead
for any signs of life and souvenirs.
Whatever he found, he took no prisoners
and always said he wondered after that
how many men he'd killed, how he'd survived.
He'd try to make some sense of all of it
but if he did, he never told us what it was.
And now he is dying of heartache and desire.
Six months into his mourning he became
an object of pursuit among the single set
of widows and divorcées hereabouts;
the hero of a joke his cronies tell
that always ends *But what a way to go!*
Last night, mistaking breathlessness for afterglow,
a woman nearly finished him with love

and barely made it to the hospital
where they thumped his chest and ordered oxygen.
The First Marines are off to war again.
He watches CNN in ICU
while leathernecks dig trenches in the sand.
The president says No More Vietnams.
The doctors tell him Easy Does It, Ed—
Six weeks, six months, who knows. It's up to you.
Avoid excitement, stimulation, sex
with any but familiar partners.
He tells them War Is Hell. It takes no prisoners.
A man must have something worth dying for.
The Persian skies are bright with bombs and fire.
My father's sleep is watched by monitors
that beep and blink—his sore heart beating, still.
I wonder if he dreams of soldiers killed
in action—Japanese, Iraqis, old Marines
who died for flags and causes, but in the end,
among their souvenirs, we only find
old snapshots of their wives and women-friends.

O GLORIOSA VIRGINUM

Truth is, I envied those pagan babies
their plentiful deities—lords in stones
and trees, goddesses of hunt and lovemaking,
their dancing liturgies in dry season.
I envied their bodies, hungry and naked,
their bare-breasted women, unbraided hair
like the women in Jimmy Shryock's magazines
with the look of knowledge on their faces.
What I wanted was to be hungry and naked
with someone, anyone, Sr. Jean Térèse,
or the dark-haired girl in the front row—*O
Gloriosa Virginum!* And yet we seemed
sublime amid the stars, somehow at odds
with our own bright bodies and our bodies' gods.

RHODODENDRONS

It was the dream
I was allowed
to touch you in.
We were strangers.
You kept your eyes closed.
I cannot really say
if there were rhododendrons
or anything like music or
even if I asked you.
Only your blue skin
and the pleasure it gave you—
the way you moved,
the way you caught your breath
whenever my hands moved
so I kept on moving them.

THAT SCREAM IF YOU EVER HEAR IT

You know who you are you
  itchy trigger-fingered sonuvabitch
  always at my elbow with your
"Rub their noses in it.
  Give it to them raw.
  Spare the cutesy metaphor and bullshit.
  Say what it was you heard or saw without
  one extra syllable."

  How some biker with a buzz-on
  doing eighty in a forty-five
  broadsides a Buick
  killing the babies buckled in the front seat
  leaving the babies' mother with a limp,
  a lengthy facial scar,
  a scream stuck in her somewhere
  north of her belly, south of her teeth.

  I know you don't need symmetry or order
  so that the biker died in pieces—
  the arm with the tattoo reading SHIT
  HAPPENS thrown a hundred yards from the one
  with NO TOMORROW on it—doesn't impress you.
  But here's a little truth
  you will approve my telling of:
  The mom is going to leave her husband,
  fight with her father,
  curse the priest.

She is going to go and live in the city,
have her face fixed, drink too much,
begin to sleep around in search
of the one and only one who can
tickle that scream out of her.

Maybe you'll run into her.
Maybe you're the one.

Here's another thing you will appreciate.
I know you'll like this. Listen up:
That scream, if you ever hear it,
won't rhyme with anything.

THE NINES

Thus we proclaim our fond affirmatives:
I will, I do, Amen, Hear hear! Let's
eat, drink and be merry. Marriage is
the public spectacle of private parts:
checkbooks and genitals, housewares, faint hearts,
all doubts becalmed by kissing aunts, a priest's
safe homily, those tinkling glasses
tightening those ties that truly bind
us together forever, dressed to the nines.

Darling, I reckon maybe thirty years,
given our ages and expectancies.
Barring the tragic or untimely, say,
ten thousand mornings, ten thousand evenings,
please God, ten thousand moistened nights like this,
when, mindless of these vows, our opposites,
nonetheless, attract. Thus, love's subtraction:
the timeless from the ordinary times—
nine thousand, nine hundred, ninety-nine.

THE LIVES OF WOMEN

A water bucket in the birthing room
to drown the female babies in is how
they do it in the outer provinces.
In other places amniocenteses gives
fair warning to the swift abortionist.
They take the tiny fetuses away
in baskets to a retort in the basement.
The smoke their bodies burning makes is hardly noticed.
In over-peopled cities, fat man-children
waddle through the streets like little emperors.
Their skinny sisters, barefoot behind them,
rummage in their litter for the leftovers.
Any survivors are taken to market
arrayed in jewels and ornamental dress—
exotic packages. The men stroll through the stalls
nodding and smiling, haggling prices.
Here in the suburbs we do it with promises
of endless protection and acts of love.
We send them to good schools and make them our muses.
We send them to market with their credit cards,
glad in their fashions and their mini-vans.
We marry them. We call them by our names.
We do the dishes and help with the children.
We ask their opinions. We nod and smile.
We keep the buckets and baskets hidden.

TOMMY

He keeps trying to replicate that day
in late September on the *Père Marquette*
when the salmon were running. How they bet
on the first fish and the most fish and the weight
of the biggest and the best. He was nine.
His mother and father were not divorced.
The salmon went upstream to spawn and die.
There seemed to be an order to the universe.
He has a picture of himself that day,
holding two cohos, looking capable.
Behind him trees are turning. It is autumn.
His mother is back home with Mike and Sean
and Heather, his sister, and all the while
his father keeps coaxing him: Smile! Smile!

WEST HIGHLAND

Whenever I hear their aged names—
Lena, Cora Mae, Lydia, Bea—
I think of prim, widowed ladies from
the Baptist church in West Highland Township;
and imagine their ordered, born-again lives
beyond the latter-day suburban sprawl
of disenchantment and convenience stores.
Lives lived out at the same pace as their mothers'
and their mothers' people years before them,
between potlucks and bake sales and bazaars,
missions and revivals, Sunday to Sunday.
And for romance, they had "Nights to Remember"—
in summer, the Bible School picnics,
October, the Farm Bureau Harvest Ball.
All winter long, they courted in parlors
with men named Thurmond or Wilbur or Russell Lloyd.
They married at Easter and bore children
and outlived their husbands and tend the graves now
after Sunday services, weather permitting.
Whenever I see them, arm in arm,
at funerals where they sing or bring baked hams
in memory of one of their sisters, dead
of the long years or the nursing home,
I think of how the century for them
was neither wars nor science nor the evening news
but a blur of careful rites of passage:
baptisms and marriages and burials.
And I envy their heavens furnished like parlors
with crocheted doilies on the davenport
and Aunt Cecelia, who never got married,

singing "In the Garden" or "Abide eith Me"
and God the Father nodding in His armchair
at saints and angels who come and go
with faces like neighbors and with names they know.

from

STILL LIFE IN MILFORD

ART HISTORY, CHICAGO

It's not so much a *Sunday Afternoon*
on the Island of La Grande Jatte as the point
of order according to Seurat—
that bits of light and color, oil paints
aligned in dots become the moment caught,
verbs slowed to a standstill, the life examined.
We step back wide-eyed for a better look:
an assemblage of Parisian suburbanites
in Sunday dress, top hats and parasols,
are there among the trees beside the river.
There are girls and women, men and dogs
in random attitudes of ease and leisure.
A stretch of beach, boats in the blue water,
a woman with a monkey on a leash,
a stiff man beside her, a mother and daughter,
that little faceless girl who seems to look at us.
And everyone is slightly overdressed except
for a boatman stretched out in the shade.
He smokes his pipe and waits for passengers.

But I have never been to Paris.
I've never holidayed beside the Seine
nor strolled with a French girl in the gray morning
as in this *Paris Street; Rainy Day*—
Gustave Caillebotte's earlier masterpiece
three galleries down in this collection.
So I do not know these cobblestones, this street,
this corner this couple seems intent on turning.
But I've walked with a woman arm in arm
holding an umbrella in a distant city,
and felt the moment quicken, yearning for
rainfall or a breeze off the river or

the glistening flesh of her body in water
the way this woman's is about to be
that Degas has painted in *The Morning Bath*.
She rises from the bed, removes her camisole,
and steps into the tub a hundred years ago.

History's a list of lovers and cities,
a mention of the weather, names and dates
of meetings in libraries and museums,
of walks by the sea or through a city,
late luncheons, long conversations, memories
of what happened or what didn't happen.
But art is the brush of a body on your body,
the permanent impression that the flesh
retains of courtesies turned intimate;
the image and likeness, the record kept
of figures emergent in oil or water
by the river, in the rain, or in the bath
when, luminous with love and its approval,
that face, which you hardly ever see,
turns its welcome toward you yet again.

KISSES

My father turns up in a dream,
sometimes on roller skates, sometimes
in wing-tipped shoes. He's smiling,
impeccably dressed, himself again.
I am delighted to see him.
Maybe I was only dreaming
is what I tell myself inside the dream.
No, he assures me wordlessly.
The facts are still the facts. He's dead.
He and my mother have been to the movies.
She's gone on ahead of him to make the coffee.
He lets me hold him, hug him,
weep some, wake repaired again,
says he'll take my kisses home to her.

BISHOP'S ISLAND

Two holy men came out here long ago
and prayed against the ground that bound them to
the green mainland and their prayers were answered.
Thus, from their rock in the North Atlantic
they watched for God among such signs and wonders
as sea and sky and wind and dark supply:
fury and firmament and privations
enough to dull the flesh, and beauty too,
to break the heart. They wept with gratitude,
kept silent, built an oratory. There,
you can see the ruins of it from the coast road.
Seabirds brought them mackerel, it is said.
Fresh water sprung from the rock. When one died
the other buried him and cut a stone,
then died himself some few years after that.
And everything was swept—his hut, his bones—
into the vast ocean and was forgot
until some bishop on a pilgrimage
centuries later, as bishops often did,
declared them saints, proclaimed the holy island His.

RENTALS LEDGER

Des Kenny up in Galway made this book
of pages fit for ink and acid-free
and sewn into a leather binding. He
put *Lynch—Moveen West* on the cover. Look
there's white space left for the likes of you.
So if you're a writer the rent is *do*.
Pay Breda Roche coin of the realm for coal
and turf, fresh linens, clean towels. The phone's
on the honor system. Pay as you go.
But leave this absentee landlord poems,
paragraphs, sentences, phrases well turned
out of your own word hoard and what you've learned.
Or better still, out of the stillness—what you hear
here in these ancient remedial stones
where Nora Lynch held forth for ninety years,
the last two decades of them on her own.
Alone by the fire in the silence she
recited the everyday mysteries
of wind and rain and darkness and the light
and sang her evening songs and sat up nights
full of wonder and reminiscences.
If you hear voices here the voice is hers.
She speaks to me still. If she speaks to you,
ready your best nib. Write what she tells you to.

AN EVENING WALK TO THE SEA BY FRIESIANS

So much in this place comes in black and white—
the cattle and clergy, magpies, the stars and dark,
those crisp arithmetics for how things are:
one for sorrow, two for joy, three to marry, four, five...
or the tally of Shalts and Thou Shalt Nots.
Despite the stars' vast evidence, we count.

A score of Michael Murray's Friesian calves
lift their faces from their pasturage
to stand and watch me standing, watching back,
my stillness and their stillness counterbalancing.
I'm making for the cliffs to fish for mackerel
to share with neighbors over evening tea.

And on these yearling hides, like seas and continents,
a random mapwork that yet articulates
a world of hard borders, sharp opposites,
clear options where the right is manifest,
the kindly husbandry of what is obvious.
Suspect of certainties, I watch the tides—

their comings and their goings, rise and fall,
the edges of approach and leave-taking
in constant motion, changing constantly
the division of ocean and landfall.
Likewise the evening light, likewise the line
between the seascape and the darkening sky

where mountains or cloudbanks or maybe islands blur
into a frontier without horizons.
God's Will, like anyone's guess at the weather,
the count we keep of certain birds, the firmament,
bright fish, the cows in their now distant fields, astray:
whatever comes in black and white goes gray.

HEAVENWARD

Such power in the naming of things—
to walk out in the greensward pronouncing
goldfinch, lilac, oriental poppy—
as if the shaping of the thing in sound
produced a pleasure like the sight of things
as if *the house finch winters in the mock-orange* is
as tasty an intelligence to the lips and ears as
the sight of a small purple bird in December
perched in a thicket of bald branches.
June you remember: *the white blossoms, yellow*
jackets, the fresh scent of heaven.
And other incarnations to be named:
nuthatch, magnolia, coreopsis, rose.
Surely this was God's first gift of godliness—
that new index finger working over the globe
assigning from the noisy void those fresh,
orderly syllables. *Ocean, garden,*
helpmate, tree of knowledge.
Making came easy, creation
a breeze. But oh, that dizzy pleasure when
God said *Eve* and the woman looked heavenward.

COUPLETS

Two girls found dead. My sons go to the morgue.
Two cots, thick rubber gloves, two body bags.

Too long stuffed in a culvert, raped and stabbed,
too decomposed to recognize. Too sad.

Two local ne'er-do-wells no doubt abused
too much as children themselves stand mute.

Two caskets in a room, two families undone.
Two ministers. Two homilies. My sons

too busy with flowers and townspeople
to contemplate the problem of evil,

to shake their fists at God, regard instead
two funerals—the living and the dead

to be transported in their separate griefs—
two hearses to be washed, two limousines.

Today the wakes and paperwork details.
Tomorrow a burning and a burial.

Two girls found dead of known brutalities
together forever, precious memories

too sweet, too savage, too beautiful and bad
to keep at bay by ritual or words.

Two boys about their father's business learn
to number, comfort, witness, and keep track.

THE MOVEEN NOTEBOOK

In memory of Nora Lynch (1902–1992)

When I first came, the old dog barked me back,
all fang and bristle and feigned attack.
I stood frozen in the road. The taxi man,
counting his crisp punt notes from Shannon, said,
"Go on boy. That's your people now." I went.
Sambo, the dog, went quiet as a bluff called.
Curtains parted in the house across the road.
The momentary sun gave way to rain.
3 February 1970—
the oval welcome in my first passport.
What kind of Yank comes in the dead of winter?
Nora stood in the doorway, figuring.

My grandfather's grandfather Patrick Lynch—
her father's father, thus, our common man—
was given this cottage as a wedding gift
when he first brought Honora Curry here
from somewhere eastern of Kilrush. Well met,
I imagine, at a cattle mart
or ceilidh dance or kinsman's wedding;
and she the grandniece of Eugene O'Curry
whose name's on the college in Carrigaholt,
accounting, according to Nora, for
any latter genius in the gene pool.
"The O'Curry breed" she would always call it
when the answer was clever, or the correct one.

As for the newlyweds, they made children:
birthed a sickly daughter and five sons here

in the first spare decade after the famines.
The names repeat themselves down generations now of
Mary Ellens, Michaels, Sinons, Dans, Pats, Toms.
And pity little: what I know of them.

Michael, the eldest boy, impregnated
one of the McMahons from across the road.
(Maybe an aunt or grand-aunt of old John Joe
who was aged when I first came here. He's dead,
the Lord've mercy on him, ten years now.)
But Michael and his pregnant neighbor wed
and moved beyond the range of gossip here
and prospered and were happy it is said
in spite of the shame of that beginning.
And Dan died young and Mary Ellen, swept
from the ledge-rocks at Doonlicky by
a freak wave when they were picking sea grass
to green the haggards with. As for Pat, the son,
he sailed to Melbourne and was never heard from
except for the tail end of a story of how
he sang from one end of the voyage
to another. "But for Lynch, we'd all do!"
it's said was said about him, his lovely tenor.
And Sinon married Mary Cunningham
and stayed here in the land—the first freehold
after centuries of British landlords.
And after Sinon died, 'twas Nora sold
eggs and new potatoes till the debt was paid
and kept her widowed mother into her age
and thereby let her own chances grow cold
for a life of men and motherhood. She stayed.
And her brother Tommy stayed and worked the land—
the loyal if withered and spinsterly end
of the line until, as Nora said, I came.

My great-grandfather sailed for Michigan—
Tomas O'Loinsigh, Nora's Uncle Tom—
and married Ellen Ryan there and worked
as a guard at Jackson Prison, pin-striped
Studebakers and lied about his age
for the warden or the factory boss or wife.
The parish house in Clare records his baptism
in 1861. The stone in Jackson's cut
1870. Either way, he died
in 1930 of the heart attack
that killed his son and killed my father after that.
And Nora, twisting these relations round, once said:
"'Twas Tom that went and Tom that would come back."

All of which might seem unnecessary now
at the end of yet another century
on the brink of this brand-new millennium
trying to set these lives and times into
Life and Time in the much larger sense:
those ineluctable modalities
that joyous man said we were given to:
how we repeat ourselves, like stars in the dark night,
and after Darwin, Freud, and Popes and worlds at war,
we are still our fathers' sons and daughters
still our mothers' darling girls and boys,
aging first, then aged, then ageless.
We bury our dead and then become them.

What kind comes in the dead of winter then?
The kind that keeps a record, names names,
says what happened, remembers certain things,
wakes the dead, leaves a witness for them after him.

So gospel or gossip, chitchat or my party piece:
a gift for my children, if they want it, this
membrance of the visit and revisiting
the stones, the fire, and the sod from which
we came, somehow, and must return again.

That first month in Moveen was wet and cold;
a fire on the floor, the open hearth,
the turf reddening against the wind that roared
up unencumbered out of Goleen Bay.
And warmed likewise against the rising damp—
that pelting daylong nightlong driven rain
that fed the puddle underneath the land.
Nora hung huge pots and kettles from the crane
and settled them into the fire coals
to boil chicken, cabbage, potatoes
or bake the soda bread or steep the tea.
Or boil water for the cow that calved
or mare that foaled or whatever hatched
in what seemed to me endless nativity
presided over by my distant cousins:
the chaste and childless aging siblings
Tommy and Nora Lynch of Moveen West
County Clare, "on the banks of the Shannon,"
my grandfather always told us—"don't forget"—
after grace was said over turkey dinners.

Tommy died in March of seventy-one.
I still can see him laid out in his bed
a rosary laced among his fingers, thumbs
curled, the purple shroud, bright coppers on his eyelids,
the missal propped between his chest and chin
as if to keep your man from giving out
with whatever the dead know that the living don't—

a tidy West Clare corpse in readiness.
Sean Collins brought the oaken coffin in
and Sonny Carmody and J. J. McMahon
and Sergeant and Tommy Hedderman
bore him on their shoulders through the yard
and out into the road where Collins' funeral car
waited with the neighbors' cars lined up behind it.
To Carrigaholt then into the cold church
where Fr. Duffy waited with his beads
and gave poor Tommy one glorious mystery
before returning to his tea and paperwork.
Next morning, Mass, then down to Pearce Fennel's
where boozy eulogists recalled the way
that Tommy would stand among his cattle
and speak to them. He called them by their names.
Or how he sang "The Boys of Kilmichael"
whenever his turn came around those nights
of talk and song and dance and old stories,
more common in the townlands years ago.
And then the slow cortege to Moyarta
beneath sufficient rain to make us quote:
"Happy is the grave the rain falls on," of course
a paltry omen in those soggy parishes.
And he was buried there among the stones,
illegible with weather, worn by wind,
his mother's bones, his brother Mikey's bones—
a tidy pile beside the grave's backfill—
together again, interred, commingled,
on the banks of the River Shannon. "Don't forget."

Thus, "Don't Forget" becomes the prayer we pray
against the moment of our leave-taking—
the whispered pleadings to our intimates,
the infant held, the lover after lovemaking,

the child who ages, the elder who
returns to childhood again. "Gone west"
is what the Clare folks call it when some old
client on the brink of dying sees
a long-dead mother in a daughter's eyes
or hears God's voice Himself in the free advice
some churchman mutters among final sacraments.
"Be stingy with the Lord and the Lord will be
stingy with you" is what Fr. Kenny said,
which was his careful way of putting forth
the theory that you get what you pay for.

So do the dead pray for remembrance as
the living do? Are these the voices that we hear
those Marchy darknesses when the whitethorn limbs
tick along the eaves and window ledges?
Or the wind hums in chimneys overhead:
or whispers to us underneath the door,
old names, old stories, old bits of wisdom?

"All winter we watch the fire," Nora said.
"All summer we watch the sea." Then she would sit
for hours hunched over, elbows to knees,
warming the palms of her hands to the fire,
smoking the cigarettes from the duty-free
shop in Kennedy I would always bring her.

"Whatever happened 'twas a freak wave took them,
above in Doonlicky and a grand fine day
and they were swept, all Lynches and O'Deas
two out of this house—a boy and girl—
and one out of Carmody's house above—
an uncle I suppose of old Kant Lynch's.

And where was the God in that I wonder?

Then rising up amid her wonderments
she'd look out westwards past the windowpane
past Sean Maloney's house gone derelict
in half a dozen winters of disuse
over hedgerow after hedgerow until her gaze
would fix on Newtown and P. J. Roche's lights
where the lap of land rose upward to the sea.

"I wonder if there's anything at all.
I wonder if He hears us when we pray."

Then chilled by her inquiries she'd sit
to stir her coals and hum "Amazing Grace,"
or give out with the names she kept alive
in the cold heaven of her memory
that tallied all but ten years of the century
the rest of us kept track of by the wars
but Nora measured by the ones she'd known:
who'd lived where, who'd married whom, who died.
And after that, who was left to grieve them.
Who waited in the land, who moved away.
Who sent home dollars. Who sent home pounds.
Who sang, who danced, who played, who drank too much.
"The cross off an ass!" is what she'd say.
Who could be trusted, who couldn't be, who lied,
and who, though dead and buried still survived
in the talk of men in public houses
or the talk of women in shops and market stalls
or the talk of neighbors at stoves or fires:
the mention of the name that keeps the name alive
and what it was they did or didn't do
to win the race or save the day or just survive—
the extraordinary moment we attribute to
them alone, irrevocably. Them only.

As, for example, how Mary Maloney,
once kicked by a cow when she was a child,
would work circles well around any man,
the limp notwithstanding. Or how she smiled.
Or the way her eyes unfailingly moistened
whenever she spoke of her dead mother.
Or how her brother Sean danced like a bull—
wide-eyed and red-faced when the music played.
Or how Dan Gorman, the Lord have mercy,
was mad for the drink and games of chance.
Or the way Kant Lynch's blinded eye
bore through me when I told him how I had
nearly been swept off the cliff at Doonlicky
by a wave that came up from the rocks behind—
a freak wave really like the hand of God—
that knocked me flat out inches from the edge.
"Mind yourself now boy," the old man said,
"the sea's ever hungry for Lynches there."
I can still see it now, near thirty years since—
the milky cataract, the thick brow arched,
the slim red warning in his good eye's squint.

As I see Johnny Hickey with his fiddle and
Denny Tubridy and his tin-whistle and
the pink Collins sisters, Bridie and Mae,
swooning in the corner to the music made
or that song Ann and Lourda Carmody sang—
Dow-n by th-e Sal-l-y gar-dens
M-y love a-nd I did meet. . .
when they were little more than little girls
singing of true romance before their time
for their elders whose moments had come and gone:
Maloneys and Murrays, Deloughreys and Downeses,

McMahons and Carmodys, Curtins and Keaneses,
Burnses and Clancys, Walshes and Lynches—
old names that fit like hand-me-downs: too loose
at times, at times too snug, sometimes all too well.
Like Theresa Murray and her sister Anne,
good neighbors who would call in on their rounds
to trade the current news, the talk in town
for Nora's ancient recollections of
the dead, the dying, and the grown or gone.

And I see Nora in the years I knew her
astride her Raleigh bike en route to town,
(One time an old dog, barking, knocked her down.
She wore the cast a week, then cut it off and
holding her hand up for inspection scoffed
"That wrist is right as paint. Three weeks? I'm healed.")
or walking with me up the coast road to
fish the mackerel or take the air or
ponder the imponderable expanse—
No parish between here and America.
We'd walk back then, with fresh fish and hunger.
Or how she battled with the Land Commission
to keep her thirty-acre heritance,
when certain neighbors had put in for it.
"Grabbers," she called them. "They want it for nothing."

"A cousin in America," she wrote,
"a young and able man is coming soon"
ten months before this unknown cousin showed
up—twentyish, unwittingly, a sign from God.
No farmer, still, I kept it in the courts
for twenty years and Nora let the land
to P. J. Roche, from Newtown, a young man
with a wife and child and a resemblance to

Tommy, the brother who had died before.
And once over pints in Mary Hickie's bar
P.J. asked me would I ever sell, if
God forbid, something should ever happen.
Take care of Nora is the thing I told him,
and I'll take care of you. The deal was cut.
So that recurring dream I'd always had
of Nora dying some night in the dark,
alone, unmissed by anyone for days,
was put to rest. P.J. and Breda kept their part
and doted over Nora like their own.
I often thought of P.J.'s evenings there—
after saving hay or dosing cattle
or maybe on the way home from the bar
he'd stop for tea, she'd put down the kettle.
He'd organize himself, then go home to Breda.
And knowing how it was, I envied that—
the quiet in the room, the way the light
went golden just before it died. The tune
she seemed always on the brink of singing,
the tiny rattle of the cups and saucers dried,
the talk between a young man and a fierce old woman.

And Nora outlived the Land Commission
and most of those who'd tried to take her land.
(One was found fell off his tractor in a ditch
and no few thought that maybe Nora's ban
was the thing that brought him to that hapless end.)
Two weeks before she died I had her will
the land outright to P.J. and his wife.
I kept the house, the haggards, and the yards,
I kept the cow-cabins, out-offices,
I kept her name in Moveen where it'd been
as far back as anyone remembered,

because I think that's what she had in mind.
And I dream you, my darling Nora, now
free of great stone vault at Moyarta
restored to the soft chair by the fire,
a kettle on, the kitten sleeping still
among the papers on the window ledge
and, maybe April, the one you never
lived to see, greening out of doors. And we
are talking in the old way, talking still,
of how the cuckoo's due here any day,
or how to count the magpies for a sign.
"A great life if you do not weaken!
And if you do. . ." you say. You turn and smile.

You approve of the hearth I had your P.J. build
of smooth gray stones drawn up from Shannonside
and how the flagstone floor was raised and thick
dampcourse put down and sand poured under it,
a window opened in the northern side,
the bathroom tiled like a French bordello
and every wall repainted *apricot*
on Mrs. Carmody's own good counsel.
You approve, likewise, of how I stir the coals
and add the sods and stare into the fire.

Is what I see there what makes me reckon
the lives we live in counterclockwise turns,
better at elegy than commencement,
better at what was done than what's to do?
To bury the dead must we first unearth them,
to see the bones still brittle in the dust,
the poor kite-work on which the poorer flesh
was hung? Is it afterward their voices
return to us in the words of others?

In the call of blackbirds or the noise of
wind and rainfall at the window sash?
Is it in their silence that the leaf-fall's
truth is spoken, the body's hunger hushed,
as last night's reddened coals turn whitened ash?
Is not the grave's first utterance, "enough, enough"?

THE OLD OPERATING THEATRE, LONDON, ALL SOUL'S NIGHT

To rooms like this old resurrectionists
returned the bodies they had disinterred—
fresh corpses so fledgling anatomists
could study Origin & Insertion points
of deltoids, pecs, trapezius and count
the vertebrae, the ball & socket joints.
And learn the private parts and Latin names
by which the heart becomes a myocardium,
the high cheek bone a zygoma, the brain,
less prone to daydream as a cerebellum.

And squirming in their stiff, unflinching seats,
apprentice surgeons witnessed, in the round,
new methods in advanced colostomy,
the amputation of gangrenous limbs,
and watched as Viennese lobotomists
banished the ravings of a raving man
but left him scarred and drooling in a way
that made them wonder was he much improved?
But here the bloodied masters taught dispassionate
incisions—how to suture and remove.

In rooms like this, the Greeks and Romans staged
their early dramas. Early Christians knelt
and hummed their liturgies when it was held
that prayer and penance were the only potions.
Ever since Abraham, guided by God,
first told his tribesmen of the deal he'd made—
their foreskins for that ancient Covenant—
good medicine's meant letting human blood.
Good props include the table and the blade.
Good theatre is knowing where to cut.

SHE INSTRUCTS THE BRETHREN ON
THE LAWS OF LOVE

You are but one in a long line of rapists
or lovers. Eventually, she will forget
the names, the faces, the earnest promises,
foreplay and afterglow. She will remember this:
how it was always a question of whether to bathe first
or first call the cops in to save the evidence.

Here is the comfort: she does not mean to hurt you.
She will hardly press charges or hold a grudge.
But do not ask Why if, after you've made love,
she weeps quietly. It is not yours to know.
Do not take it personally. Roll over.
Go to sleep. It has nothing to do with you.

STILL LIFE IN MILFORD—OIL ON CANVAS
BY LESTER JOHNSON

You're lucky to live in a town like this
with art museums and Indian food
and movie houses showing foreign films
and grad students and comely undergrads.
Years back I'd often make the half-hour trip.
It was good for my creative juices
to browse the holy books at Shaman Drum.
Still, life in Milford isn't all that bad.

We have two trendy restaurants and a bar
well known by locals for its Coney dogs.
We have a book shop now. We even have
a rush hour, art fairs, and bon vivants.
And a classic car show every October—
mostly muscle cars—Dodges, Chevys, Fords.
No psychic healers yet or homeopaths.
Still, life in Milford has a certain ambience,

more Wyeth than Picasso, to be sure,
more meatloaf and potatoes than dim-sum. Fact is,
at first I thought this Lester Johnson was
a shirt-tail cousin of the Johnson brothers—
long-standing members of the Chamber of Commerce
in Milford, Michigan, like me. In fact
his only connection to these parts was
Still Life in Milford, gathering dust here

in the basement of the art museum.
His own Milford's somewhere back east, near Yale—
the day job, teaching, he could never quit
the way that Robert Frost taught English here
and Donald Hall before the muse in them
escaped their offices in Angell Hall.
They were last seen running and maybe running still.
Life in Milford, Michigan, is similar.

I have steady work, a circle of friends
and lunch on Thursdays with the Rotary.
I have a wife, unspeakably beautiful,
a daughter and three sons, a cat, a car,
good credit, taxes and mortgage payments
and certain duties here. Notably,
when folks get horizontal, breathless, still:
life in Milford ends. They call. I send a car.

Between the obsequies I play with words.
I count the sounds and syllables and rhymes.
I try to give it shape and sense, like so:
eight stanzas of eight lines apiece, let's say
ten syllables per line or twelve. Just words.
And if rhyming's out of fashion, I fashion rhymes
that keep their distance, four lines apart, like so.
Still, life in Milford keeps repeating. Say

I'm just like Lester, just like Frost and Hall:
I covet the moment in which nothing moves
and crave the life free of life's distractions.
A bucket of flowers on a table.
A vase to arrange the flowers in. A small
pipe—is it?—smoldering in an ashtray to
suggest the artist and impending action.
Still Life in Milford seems a parable

on the human hunger for creation.
The flowers move from bucket to vase
like moving words at random into song—
the act of ordering is all the same—
the ordinary becomes a celebration.
Whether paper, canvas, ink, or oil paints,
once finished we achieve a peace we call
Still Life in Milford. Then we sign our names.

from

WALKING PAPERS

EUCLID

What sort of morning was Euclid having
when he first considered parallel lines?
Or that business about how things equal
to the same thing are equal to each other?
Who's to know what the day has in it?
This morning Bert took it into his mind
to make a long bow out of Osage orange
and went on eBay to find the cow horns
from which to fashion the tips of the thing.
You better have something to pass the time
he says, stirring his coffee, smiling.
And Murray is carving a model truck
from a block of walnut he found downstairs.
Whittling away he thinks of the years
he drove between Detroit and Buffalo
delivering parts for General Motors.
Might he have nursed theorems on lines and dots
or the properties of triangles or
the congruence of adjacent angles?
Or clearing customs at Niagara Falls,
arrived at some insight on wholes and parts
or an axiom involving radii
and the making of circles, how distance
from a center point can be both increased
endlessly and endlessly split—a mystery
whereby the local and the global share
the same vexations and geometry?
Possibly this is where God comes into it,
who breathed the common notion of coincidence
into the brain of that Alexandrian
over breakfast twenty-three centuries back,
who glimpsed for a moment that morning the sense

it all made: life, killing time, the elements,
the dots and lines and angles of connection—
an egg's shell opened with a spoon, the sun's
connivance with the moon's decline, Sophia
the maidservant pouring juice; everything,
everything coincides, the arc of memory,
her fine parabolas, the bend of a bow,
the curve of the earth, the turn in the road.

MONTBRETIA

for Michael O'Connell

Montbretia blooming up the Moveen Road,
never native to the flora hereabouts,
arrived more than a hundred years ago
when sons of the Dutch-born landlord both went out
to fight for the crown in the Boer Wars.
One was killed. One came home with flowers—
this orangey iris from South Africa,
named for a botanist somewhere in France
who was named for the hill that he called home
a century before. It was ever thus—
from the place, a people; from the mass, particulars:
this tribe, this kind, this crowd, this sort, not that.
From all of time, this late July, this moment;
from every other one, this one and only.
Especially we name the wars and flowers,
the chieftains and discoverers, gods and lovers.
So: *crocosmia, crocosmiiflora*
from the family Iridaceae—
those subdividing tongues and etymologies,
those lists and plots, old myths and litanies.
The seedling planted in the great-house garden
leapt the stone walls of the Vandeleurs
in the beak of a bird, on gardener's boot or breeze
and spread through Kilrush, round Poulnasherry
and out the townlands of the estuary,
all the way to Loop Head where West Clare ends,
and where some western in his anecdotage,
accounting for the rock off that peninsula—
that limestone tower, that god-awful keening—
fashioned a story of star-crossed lovers

who, running from love's grievous binding knot,
or striving for some distant privacy,
leapt the chasm to the tiny island.
One version holds they both leapt back again.
One made it and one fell to death, withal
we've named whatever perched or nested there:
storm petrel, common tern, and herring gull,
Dermot and his Grainne, Cuchulain, and Mal,
shearwater, fulmer, *Larus argentatus*.
Thus, Loop Head is the place where lovers leapt
and found, like wars and flowers, everything
repeats itself—the setting out, the settling in,
the loop unwound winds up itself again;
the story, the screech of seabirds, the voice of gods,
in every leap some landing and some fall;
the seed, the stone: in every start an end.

FR. ANDREWS

Jake, for the record, life does go on. Tuesday
gives way to Wednesday unremarkably.
The stars in their firmament behave like stars.
The morning traffic makes its mindless way
from one preoccupation to another.
Little changes. You knew as much yourself:
we have our day and others after us,
into their sparkling moment and out beyond.
We have our little say and then are silent.
But still, you met the mourners at the door,
and pressed the heavens with their lamentations
and tried to make some sense of all of it,
then saw them to the edge and home again—
the way we see you now, our level man,
out of the morning's worship into the sun,
the coach at the curb, and on your way again.

TO BE AMONG THESE ELEGANT VOICES

This image of the plump-faced peasantry
all knees and codpieces dancing round
someplace in Belgium at a wedding I found
among the *B*'s in *Artists—European*.
The way the book is printed, how it's bound
is a matter of indifference to me.
I want what's in it—the thousand words' worth
on every page—the contemplation
of its creator's life and times, the memory
of the moment I first beheld it
in Detroit, at the Institute of Arts
with that bookish girl I was trying to get,
as we used to say then, biblical with.
Was it 1970? Was it April?
Was she as lovely as I remember?
Was it "Yes, that's it, oh yes" she whispered?
Or have I confused her with another?
But wait—the place is full of echoes now.
Across the room among the *W*'s
in *English Romantic Poetry* Words-
worth is pacing out his iambic tune:
The child is Father of the man. . .
his footfall sounding in the garden's gravel,
while Keats and Coleridge proceed uphill.
Or maybe it's that one word—"biblical"—
that sets us rummaging through the scriptures.
Job, that long-suffering protagonist,
hapless, damaged, put upon by friends—
"Blessed be the name of the Lord," he yet insists
in that vexing, god-awful, answerless book.
It disturbed his people and disturbs us still.
"Sometimes," says Alan Dugan in a poem,

"Disturbed people go to the public library. . ."
He's right, of course, books can make us crazy,
or give us hope, or make us question things.
Where else but in our public library
can we indulge our curiosities,
imagination dancing in the round,
as one notion chases after others?
To be among these elegant voices
can get you going off in all directions
and get you back somehow from whence you came.
Take this place, for example, all these choices:
Hobbies, *Reference Books*, *Biography*,
Fiction, *Magazines*, all these places, people, names
shelved and silenced alphabetically,
some dead and gone, still singing all the same.
Emily Dickinson, Mark Twain, James Joyce
whose Molly and Leopold, whose Huckleberry,
whose *After great pain a formal feeling comes*
become sweet fodder for our hungry minds,
or common guidance for our ruminations,
timely as the moments we occupy.
Today's the eighth of June. What else is new?
My wife and I are going to a wedding.
The world's supply of heartache is secure.
There's love and hate and mayhem everywhere.
We've come to dedicate some space to words,
some rooms for visions and remembrances.
It's good to look through windows on the world
from a corner of a quiet place. Good
to keep the records and corrected texts,
histories and newspapers and ancient tracts
of what we human beings were doing here.
I was just browsing in *American Poets*
to find some good words for the nuptials—

some verse by which to toast the newlyweds—
when I came across this poem called "The Dance"
by William Carlos Williams. What it says
about the *tweedle of bagpipes*, about
a bugle and fiddles and *rollicking measures*
and *Breughel's great picture The Kermess*
makes me grateful for the things we find in books:
this painting of peasants dancing in Flanders,
the poems on paintings and marriages;
the books they're in, the places where the books are kept.

CORPSES DO NOT FRET THEIR COFFIN BOARDS

after Wordsworth

Corpses do not fret their coffin boards,
nor bodies wound in love their narrow beds:
size matters less to lovers and the dead
than to the lonely and the self-absorbed
for whom each passing moment is a chore
and space but vacancy: unholy dread
of what might happen or not happen next;
this dull predicament of less or more's
a never-balanced book, whereas for me,
the worth of words is something I can count
out easily, on fingertips—the sounds
they make, the sense, their coins and currencies—
these denouements doled out in tens, fourteens:
last reckonings tapped out on all accounts.

OH SAY GRIM DEATH

No doubt the Reverend Ainsworth read from Job
Over the charred corpse of the deacon's boy
To wit: "Blessed be the name of the Lord"
Or some such comfortless dose of holy writ
That winter morning after the house fire
Put all the First Congregationalists
Of Jaffrey Center, New Hampshire,
Out weeping and gnashing, out in the snow
While the manse at Main Street and Gilmore Pond Road
Blazed into the early Thursday morning.
God's will is done as often without warning
As with one. Either way, *Revere His laws*
Is cut into the child's monument
To rhyme with a previous sentiment:
Cease, Man, to ask the hidden cause. As if
The answers ever were forthcoming. So
Little's known of young *Isaac A. Spofford*—
His father, *Eleazar*, his mother, *Mary*,
His death on the *thirteenth of February*
In *Seventeen Hundred Eighty-eight.*
A brand plucked from the ashes reads the stone
Of Rev. Laban Ainsworth's house; which frames
The sadness in the pastor's burning faith,
In God's vast purposes. As if the boy
Long buried here was killed to show how God
Makes all things work together toward some good.
And yet the stone's inquiry still haunts:
Oh say, grim death why thus destroy
The parents' hopes, their fondest joy—
Or say, instead, grim death destroys us all
By mighty nature's witless, random laws

Whereby old churchmen, children, everything—
All true believers, all who disbelieve,
Come to their ashen ends and life goes on.

THE LIFE OF FICTION

Everything must, of course, advance the cause
of atmosphere or character or narrative:
the walk up the coast road, the sudden rain,
the stone shed at the sea's edge to shelter in,
the two of them waiting out the weather,
pressed into the corner, alone at last.
This is an old movie. It's Hollywood.
Each gets to tell the other everything—
old dreams and longings, slow regrets, how things
happen as they are supposed to happen,
or so they will console each other.
Of course, the usual embraces. They smile and weep.
They touch each other's faces wordlessly,
then step out into the eventual sun,
each knowing what the other wanted known.
Or here's another possibility:
It doesn't rain. Or when it does,
a helpful pilgrim happens by and shouts,
"Hop in, you'll be perished, I'll get you home!"
And they get back safely, dry and comforted,
grateful for their dispensations. Life goes on.
The sea and the weather keep coming and going.

AFTER YOUR GOING

There was this hollow after your going
as if the air you'd lately occupied,
having waited for you these long years, sighed
at your leaving; as if the light were lonely
and the day bereft and the evening lost
without your habitation, and the room,
once you vacated it, returned to stone
and fire and a chair and the old ghosts.

THIRTEEN FOR SEAN AT THIRTY

It was on this day in 1496
Da Vinci tried out his flying machine.
It failed; he crashed, but kept hard at it.
Helicopters, parachutes, ornithopters—
birdlike contraptions that fell to earth
as all must do, with thud and bruises.
God knows some days we all feel like losers.
The heart, it turns out, like a leaf in autumn,
like Leonardo, that 3rd of January,
between swoon and sure damage, rapture and doom,
never a stasis, and yet we fly, uncertain
if we're coming or going or whether we've gone
partway in the journey or partway home.

DEAR MR. PRESIDENT

The black cow we put inside
for Mrs. Murray to inseminate
got its head stuck in the metal gate
and couldn't get it out.
What was she thinking?
we said to each other.
Talk about a rock and a hard place.
Maybe it swelled some
after she forced it through.
Still, we couldn't get it out
though we kicked with our boots,
twisted it every which way,
cursed, swore, shouted, prayed.
Nothing worked.
The thing was stuck
and we were stuck with it.
How could we go back to our lives
with that beast out there,
its fat head caught in the gate?
We couldn't go to church
or the movies or the store.
What would we say when folks asked,
how are things? As they do.
In the end we had to get a saw—
one of those big round yokes
that make an awful noise
and cut through anything.
After everything we just cut it out—
it was that simple, Mr. President—
we just cut it out.
One clean cut at the corner,
bent it open until she pulled

her thick head out and stood there looking
like cows do, you know,
blameless, serviceable, and dull,
just in time for the bull,
which comes in a suitcase now,
says Mrs. Murray, the inseminator,
wearing a blue rubber glove
all the way up to her shoulder
pushing deep inside that beast,
all the while looking
up into the high roof joists of the shed
where swallows were nesting.
The look on her face—Mrs. Murray's—
was, I have to tell you Mr. President,
so sublime, so beautiful.
We said there is a science to everything.

LOCAL HEROES

Some days the worst that can happen happens.
The sky falls or evil overwhelms or
the world as we have come to know it turns
toward the eventual apocalypse
long predicted in all the holy books—
the end-times of old grudge and grievances
that bring us each to our oblivions.
Still, maybe this is not the end at all,
nor even the beginning of the end.
Rather, one more in a long list of sorrows
to be added to the ones thus far endured,
through what we have come to call our history—
another in that bitter litany
that we will, if we survive it, have survived.
God help us who must live through this, alive
to the terror and open wounds: the heart
torn, shaken faith, the violent, vengeful soul,
the nerve exposed, the broken body so
mingled with its breaking that it's lost forever.
Lord send us, in our peril, local heroes.
Someone to listen, someone to watch, someone
to search and wait and keep the careful count
of the dead and missing, the dead and gone
but not forgotten. Some days all that can be done
is to salvage one sadness from the mass
of sadnesses, to bear one body home,
to lay the dead out among their people,
organize the flowers and casseroles,
write the obits, meet the mourners at the door,
drive the dark procession down through town
toll the bell, dig the hole, tend the pyre.
It's what we do. The daylong news is dire—

full of true believers and politicos,
bold talk of holy war and photo ops.
But here, brave men and women pick the pieces up.
They serve the living, caring for the dead.
Here the distant battle is waged in homes.
Like politics, all funerals are local.

DEAR MR. VICE PRESIDENT

It was one cow trying to
mount the other—
"bulling" they call it hereabouts,
though in fairness
the bull was nowhere to be found—
just one black-and-white cow
with a pink udder
and its own agenda
trying to mount another,
for reasons unknown to your
humble correspondent,
that fractured the latter's hindquarters
so it lay out in the high meadow,
looking oafish and put upon.
It couldn't move or graze,
couldn't make its way to water.
It made for itself an awful noise—
that low-grade plaint
cows make while calving,
but worse somehow: a hopeless case.
Squinting upland through his window
J.J. could make out something wrong.
He tractored it down into the
haggard to tend to it, bringing it
fresh grass, sups of water, carrying on
the mindless conversations
humans have with larger mammals.
For days it just lay there
shitting itself, making its lament,
J.J. hoping it might find its way
back into the brutish world
nature had assigned to it.

He spoke to the priest
and lit a candle. He called the vet
who came and had a look.
But it was broken. That was obvious.
It was going nowhere.
He sent for Coffey then
who came with his truck
rigged with a crane and length of cable.
After putting a kill shot
between its eyes, Coffey hoist it
into the gray evening air.
That moment it hung there in the sky,
Mr. Vice President,
the deadweight mass of its disaster,
its limbs akimbo,
the glaze of its eyes,
its bestial ruination pure,
the misery it was so
suddenly out of—
all of it put me in mind
of the charred corpses
of those men they strung
from the bridge that time
after dragging them
through the mob and town—
that silhouette of broken parts
twisted by gravity and damage
into misdirection.
"Ah hell," J.J. said,
"it's entirely fucked."
Disconsolate,
Mr. Vice President,
that is the word
that came into my brain

when J.J. said
"Ah hell" again,
and again "it's fucked."
Then went inside
and closed his door
to everything out there
where he had been.

HIMSELF

He'll have been the last of his kind here then.
The flagstones, dry-stone walls, the slumping thatch,
out-offices and cow cabins, the patch
of haggard he sowed spuds and onions in—
all of it a century out of fashion—
all giving way to the quiet rising damp
of hush and vacancy once he is gone.
Those long contemplations at the fire, cats
curling at the door, the dog's lame waltzing,
the kettle, the candle and the lamp—
all still, all quenched, all darkened—
the votives and rosaries and novenas,
the pope and Kennedy and Sacred Heart,
the bucket, the basket, the latch and lock,
the tractor that took him into town and back
for the pension check and messages and pub,
the chair, the bedstead and the chamber pot,
everything will amount to nothing much.
Everything will slowly disappear.
And some grand-niece, a sister's daughter's daughter,
one blue August in ten or fifteen years
will marry well and will inherit it:
the cottage ruins, the brown abandoned land.
They'll come to see it in a hired car.
The kindly Liverpudlian she's wed,
in concert with a local auctioneer,
will post a sign to offer SITE FOR SALE.
The acres that he labored in will merge
with a neighbor's growing pasturage
and all the decades of him will begin to blur,
easing, as the far fields of his holding did,
up the hill, over the cliff, into the sea.

DEAR MADAM SECRETARY

It was the bucket of oats
I was giving the mare ass
that gave her wee she-foal the shits—
out there in the haggard
gazing at the wall
incomprehensibly,
the green ooze
staining her rear flanks,
her entire aspect badly shaken.
Milk scours—P.J. diagnosed it—
and sent me to Williams,
the chemist in town,
for a big syringe
and some sort of dose
to restore the poor creature's
proper fettle.
It was pink—the dose was—
and it smelled like berries.
Mornings and evenings
we'd bring her inside,
and get her to
suckle a finger or thumb,
then plunge the medicine
down her throat.
In no time she was
out gamboling in the
sweet grass, pulling at
the pink dugs of the mare ass,
good, we figured, for donkey's years.
Not so the painful case
of a weanling Friesian
that got a chill

from the cold rain
of a late June night—
out in the low field,
down and wheezing.
Pneumonia, we figured
and could only hope
the injection we gave it
would save the thing.
I found it in the shed
the following morning,
dead as any specimen
has ever been.
And what I wanted
to share with you Madam Secretary,
out there with the shovel,
digging the grave,
is that husbandry
has its disappointments.
What I am trying to say
is that the way of things
will not be tampered with.
Or, as one of your
colleagues once opined,
"stuff happens."
Surely what he meant to say
was shit, Madam Secretary.
It's shit that happens.
Ask any ass.

ON A BAR OF CHINESE SOAP

The way the bee and flower on this bar
of Chinese soap will suds into a blur
of common form and purpose is not far
from how in due course memory obscures
the edges of what happened and what didn't.
In time it's all befuddlement: names, dates,
loves, hates, what in fact was said, what wasn't.
And thus this slow immersion compensates,
this laving of the body and the mind,
this anointing by both bee and flower
from which we're left at length to rise, alive,
cleansed, buzzing and fragrant, free of the dire
consequence of time, the dour habits
of the heart, the sore flesh it so inhabits.

DEAR MESSRS. ATTORNEYS GENERAL

It's living on the cliff road
makes it easy—what's done
with surplus kittens hereabouts
or yelping collies once
the bitch has whelped,
involving a sack, a rock,
the cover of nightfall
or early morning.
Times like these,
as you know yourselves,
Messrs. Gonzales and Mukasey,
require such extremes.
Here on the frontlines
it's all we can manage,
any day, any one of us,
to handle the dispatches.
And if the ends do not
justify the means, still,
ends are what we're after. Nonetheless,
there's something to behold—
May I call you Alberto?
May I call you Michael?—
Something wondrous in the
rendition of the thing:
the kicking bundle swung into oblivion,
the arc of its descent,
the great gulp of the ocean over it,
the cleanly disappearance, not a trace,
not a quibble, not a corpse;
everything, even the memory of it,
swept away in the wind and tide.

The Prevention of Cruelty crowd
have the law on their side, lads.
But we have order.

WALKING PAPERS

to Michael Heffernan

I reckoned reading Frost would put you right
and making something from a line of his
a better way to use what's left of time
than trying to diagnose what's killing you—
something your doctor said about something
he gathered from something in your latest labs,
letting slip some quibble about blood work
or enzymes or liver function. Listen—
something's going to get you in the end.
The numbers are fairly convincing on this,
hovering, as they do, around a hundred
percent. We die. And more's the pity.
Same for the goose as for the gander, true
for both saints and sinners, fit and fat.
We get our dose of days and after that
we get whatever is or isn't next:
heaven, remembered, a kick in the ass,
a place in a frame on some grandkid's piano,
a grave, a tomb, the fire, our ashes scattered,
the scavenging birds, the deep, nirvana—
sure, one oblivion's good as another.
By all accounts there's nothing to it, pal—
a cake walk, kicked bucket, falling off a log;
one moment you are and next you aren't,
the way that semicolon slipped in there
before the comma in the following line
three lines before the coming period.
You can think of it as punctuation
and maybe take some comfort from that, friend—
a question mark or exclamation point—

no matter, we're all sentenced to an end,
the movers and the shakers, bon vivants,
all ne'er-do-wells and nincompoops, savants,
sage and sluggard, deft and daft alike:
everyone's given their walking papers.
Everyone's shown the door and sees the light.
The adverbials are incidental,
dull as any devil in the details
and though the eulogists are reverential
once it's over no one gives a wrap
whether tumor, tantrum, stroke or heart attack,
too many cigarettes, too-frenzied sex,
too many cheeseburgers, too old an age,
a murderous shellfish or tsunami swept
the creature from creation's little stage,
waving and smiling, kicking and screaming,
at ease or agonizing, anyway,
the hush, the breathlessness, it's all the same.
The month, the day, the year, the proper names,
the size of the stone, what gets cut in it—
I had a lovers' quarrel with the world.
Enough's enough. Good riddance. Less is more.
I told you that I wasn't feeling good!
Together wing to wing and oar to oar—
but footnotes to insuperable truth:
we mortals come with our mortalities,
freighted, laden, born with our last breath in us.
Why worry whether this or that improves
or ruins your chances. No guarantees
come with our particular models—we
get our final markdowns, deep discounts:
a coupon good for nothing more or less.
So quit the medicos and pharmacists,
who've got a pill for whatever ails you—

restless leg or ornery bowel,
a lapsed erection, cauliflower ears,
sugar, tapeworm, loose stools, septicemia—
I say clean your plate and say your prayers,
go out for a long walk after supper
and listen for the voice that sounds like you
talking to yourself, you know the one:
contrapuntal, measured to footfall, true
to your own metabolism. Listen—
inspiration, expiration, it's all the same,
the sigh of creation and its ceasing—
whatever's going to happen's going to happen.
Who knows the number when your number's up?
So, go on out and count some syllables,
lay some lines down one after another,
check the pulses, make the meters tick,
make up whatever noise you have to make
to make some sense of the day that's in it.
I have my doubts on almost everything.
I sit in church and think these hooligans
are only fellow pilgrims, like myself,
no more beatific than a heap of bones,
lost and grinning for no apparent reason.
That said, I've had these glimpses, inklings,
sometimes it's almost as if I'm haunted.
Things come to me as apparitions do.
My late father, for instance, my dear mother,
just now that fellow Frost you like to quote,
they often reappear in lines like these
as if they had a message meant for me
which echoes with a thing I've always known:
Life goes on. Forever. It's impossible.
Remember when it cost just fourteen cents
to send a sonnet on an index card?

"The postal service imitating art"—
which one of us said that, my lettered friend?
And now we carry on page after page
as if we both depended on it still.
We carry on and pay the going rate
because we keep as articles of faith
there might be something for us in the mail.
God knows we could turn up, the two of us,
long after our long correspondence goes
silent as all such correspondents must.
Maybe someone will get some wind of us
in some old book or in the bonfire,
the firebug rising to its occasion,
the way the frost appears, then disappears,
a door that swings both ways on its hinges. . .
It could happen. We could go on forever.
If so we'll want a codeword, secret sign,
something to make it known we recognize
each other. How about "New Hampshire?"
How 'bout we grab our groins or give a wave,
like third -ase coaches when the count is full,
to signal *take a pitch* or *guard the plate*,
go for the walk or *runner stealing home*?
To signal all is well, we're not alone,
we'll both of us turn over in our graves.

CALLING

We Catholic boys all listened for The Call.
The Voice of God, exquisite in our ears—
Come follow me, or, as it was with Paul,
Thunder, enlightening, the bang and whisper
By which God makes His will known to us all.
Be fruitful. But not apples. Is that clear?

Or as it was with Noah, *Build an ark.*
Or Abraham, *Prove your faith, man, kill your boy.*
Or Moses, *So you're thirsty? Smite the rock.*
Or Job, out of the whirlwind, *Gird your loins.*
Or that fervent girl-child, Joan of Arc,
Who burned but never renounced her "voices."

Belief is easy when God speaks to us.
The ordinary silence—there's the thing—
The soul-consuming quiet, the heavens' hush
That sets even the pious wondering.
Lord spare us all, we doubting Thomases,
Who, even with a trembling finger in

The wound, still ask aloud, "My Lord? My God?"
Ever curious, too inquisitive.
I was named after a "Fr. Tom"—
My father's uncle, Thomas Patrick Lynch,
A sickly boy who died before his time,
(1904—1936)

Saving Apaches at Rancho de Taos
Breathing some easier that rarified air
Of the Sangre de Christo Mountains.
The blood of Christ, when he was done, ran clear.

Once in the basement of my grandparents' house
I found his cassock and Roman collar

Hanging from a rafter, blessed and bodiless
And under it, a trunk of priestly things,
Surplice and biretta, bright chalices,
A sick call kit and leather breviary.
I tried them all. Though nothing seemed to fit,
All the same, I kept on listening.

And I served at altar for our parish priest,
The Reverend Thomas Kenny—never "Tom,"
Never wavering, never doubtful in the least—
A Holy Roman Irish Catholic man
Who lost his bearings when they Englished everything,
Like Barry Fitzgerald or Fr. Flanagan.

After morning Masses, he'd make me kneel
For half an hour in the back of church
To offer thanksgiving for the holy meal
I was after having in the Eucharist.
"Be stingy with the Lord, boyo, and He'll
Be stingy in return." He kept a list

Of saints and shortcomings, shalts and shalt-nots,
Mortal, venial, deadly, and cardinal sins,
Contrary virtues, graces, gifts of God,
The glorious and sorrowful mysteries,
Holy days, first Fridays, stations of the Cross,
Corporal and spiritual works of mercy.

It was a language I learned to speak,
Lovely and Latin, a sort of second tongue—
My parents' and people's, the nuns' and priests'—

That rose in the air like incense and song
Ghostly and Gregorian, like memories:
First gushing, then going, but never gone.

And I am listening, listening still.
"We're given two ears and one mouth for good reason.
Pray to know God's purpose and you will."
So said the old priest, and I believed him.
"*Carpe momentum*, boy—each minute is a gift."
And though I wonder still, sometimes I seize it.

Sometimes I see that dead priest in my dreams
In the basement of Desnoyer's Funeral Home
In Jackson, Michigan—he's on the table.
The train has brought him home from Santa Fe.
Two men in shirtsleeves vest and casket him
While my father, just gone twelve, stands in the door

Unnoticed, watching, watching everything.
Upstairs his father's organizing things—
The flowers, Mass and burial, a stone.
The fifth of August 1936:
That Wednesday morning when our dad was "called"—
Or so he always told us after that—

To this life's work between the quick and dead.
And so we do, these generations since,
My brothers, sisters, sons and daughter, all
Carry on as if we'd heard it too—
That silence or that summons—who's to know
Whether faith moves mountains or if mountains move?

REFUSING AT FIFTY-TWO TO WRITE SONNETS

It came to him that he could nearly count
How many Octobers he had left to him
In increments of ten or, say, eleven
Thus: sixty-three, seventy-four, eighty-five.
He couldn't see himself at ninety-six—
Humanity's advances notwithstanding
In health care, self-help, or New Age regimens—
What with his habits and family history,
The end he thought is nearer than you think.

The future, thus confined to its contingencies,
The present moment opens like a gift:
The balding month, the gray week, the blue morning,
The hour's routine, the minute's passing glance—
All seem like godsends now. And what to make of this?
At the end the word that comes to him is Thanks.

from

THE SIN-EATER: A BREVIARY

THE SIN-EATER

Argyle the sin-eater came the day after—
a narrow, hungry man whose laughter
and the wicked upturn of his one eyebrow
put the local folks in mind of trouble.
But still they sent for him and sat him down
amid their whispering contempts to make
his table near the dead man's middle,
and brought him soda bread and bowls of beer
and candles, which he lit against the reek
that rose off that impenitent cadaver
though bound in skins and soaked in rosewater.
Argyle eased the warm loaf right and left
and downed swift gulps of beer and venial sin,
then lit into the bread now leavened with
the corpse's cardinal mischiefs, then he said
"Sixpence, I'm sorry." And the widow paid him.
Argyle took his leave then, down the land
between hayricks and Friesians with their calves
considering the innocence in all
God's manifold creation but for Man,
and how he'd perish but for sin and mourning.
Two parishes between here and the ocean:
a bellyful tonight is what he thought,
please God, and breakfast in the morning.

ARGYLE IN AGONY

Some sins Argyle couldn't stomach much.
Sins against virgin girls and animals,
women bearing children, men gone blind
from all but self-abusive reasons gave him
stomach troubles, like over-seasoned meat
he oughtn't to have eaten, but he always did.
Some nights those evils woke him in his sleep,
gaseous and flatulent, bent over his puke bowl,
resolved again to draw the line somewhere,
to leave the dirty work to younger men,
or anyway, to up his prices.
Maybe steady work with nuns whose vices
were rumored to go down like tapioca.
But no, those clever ladies lived forever
and for all their charities would starve the man
who counted for his feed on their transgressions.
Better to go on as he always had,
eating sins and giving souls their blessed rest.
What matter that his innards heaved against
a steady diet of iniquities
or that children worked their mayhem on his head
by carving pumpkins up in fearful effigies?
He had his holy orders and his mission.
He had the extreme unction of his daily bread.

ARGYLE'S VAPORS

Vaporous and sore at heart, Argyle
stood in his doorway looking out at nothing.
The wind blew through him as if he wasn't.
As if he were, himself, a door ajar
through which one had to go to get nowhere
and wanting to go nowhere, there he stood—
a spectacle of shortfall and desire.
And all the voice of reason in him reasoned was
"Take heart, Argyle! This is seasonal.
The winter is a cruel but equal cross
borne only by the living in the name of Christ,
and though a cold encumbrance on the soul afire
with ministry and purpose, bear in mind
the dead will keep for days in such weather
and any climate so kind to a corpse
will shorten purgatory for those left alive
to huddle in their mud and wattles for some warmth."
Such comfort as that gave him helped him weather
well enough the chill and shortened days,
the noise of rats wintering in his thatch,
the endless bitter merriment at wakes.
By dark he dreamt the touch of female flesh—
all night in sweats and brimming scenes of pleasure—
and waking up alone, he blamed the weather.

ARGYLE'S BALANCE

Argyle kept his balance feeling himself
between two equal and opposing forces,
each, at once, both fearsome and endearing.
He had dreams. In one a woman in her bright flesh
kneels in the river, bathing. Later, she
lies in the tall grass drying, reddening
her nipples with the juice of pomegranates,
offering them and her body to him.
This was his dream of youth and lovemaking,
of greensong, water, all life-giving things.
The other was a dream of himself, in
extremis. The children gather, dumbstruck
at his belly, bulbous with flatus, fat
with the old sins of others and his own.
A priest stands ready with chrisms and forgiveness.
He always dreamt this after radishes.
These were the horizontal mysteries
from either one of which he would arise
breathless with intimacy and release,
invigored with deliverance, alive.
The answer he figured was to keep an arm's reach
between his waking self and either dream, listing
only slightly from upright anytime
the dreams made music and he would listen.

ARGYLE'S EJACULATIONS

Argyle's preference in sins was legend.
The best of them were those the priests invented:
broken fasts or abstinence in Lent,
a tithe unpaid or Sunday morning passed
in honest, gainful labor or in bed.
He feasted full on Easter Duties missed
or some bad-mouthing of a Jesuit.
He relished churchy sins that had no flesh
or blood or bones, but only upset
some curate's dictum on moral etiquette.
"God Bless His Holiness in Rome, O Lord!"—
Argyle often ejaculated—
"And all Right Reverend Eminence & Graces,
and all the idle time they have to kill
concocting new sins for my evening meal."
But then he'd dream that girl-child again,
defiled by some mannish violence who threw
herself to death, despairing, down a bog hole.
And when the parish house refused her requiems,
her people sent for Argyle to come
and undo by his dinner what the girl had done.
But Argyle knelt and wept and refused the bread,
and poured the bowl of bitters on the ground
and prayed, "God spare my hunger till that churchman's dead."

ARGYLE'S RETREAT

Great hosts of basking sharks and shoals of mackerel,
like brethren in the one Creation, swam
together in the seas around Loop Head Point,
free of those long-standing habits of predation
whereby the larger fellow eats the small.
In Kilkee church, two girls saw statues move.
Lights appeared and disappeared and reappeared
from Doonaghboy to Newtown and the dead were seen
perched upon ditchbanks with their turnip lamps by night.
In Moveen, cattle sang, crows barked, and kittens flew.
The tidal pools at Goleen filled with blood
and all the common wisdoms were undone
by signs and wonders everywhere. Argyle
wondered were they miracles or omens?
God's handiwork or some bedevilment
called up or down on him by that avenging priest
he'd lately tangled with? Either way, *retreat*
was the word that formed in him. A fortnight's rest
at Dingle, fast and prayer to purge and cleanse himself
among those holy hermits there who never
once, for all their vast privations, ever
saw or heard a thing or apprehended God
abounding in their stars or stones or seas.
And for all they hadn't witnessed, yet believed.

ARGYLE'S DREAM OF THE CHURCH DOVE

Argyle saw the Inner Hebrides
in dreams and dozings, spasms of the light
in which the vision under eyelids brightened
the dark precincts of ancient memory.
Iona in his father's father's time. . .
His father's father singing to the sea
a lamentation of his own mad making
aside the strand where blessed Columcille
first landed with his boats and brother monks
and looking back from Ulster couldn't see
beyond the thickening pale of exile.
O ancient gray-eyed saint—the old one sang—
old sire of my bastard lineage,
please intercede with God to send a Sign
that I might know my bilious ministry
serves both the sinner and The Sinned Against!
At that a church dove flew out of the fog
and striving skyward shat upon his head,
the bird's anointing oozing into each
and every sensing orifice he had.
And shaken by the vision, Argyle,
uncertain of its meaning, nonetheless
woke mouthing words of praise and wonderment
in fiery tongues, remarkable and strange.

ARGYLE IN CARRIGAHOLT

At Carrigaholt the priest was famous for
the loud abhorrence that he preached against
adherence to the ancient superstitions.
Old cures, evil eyes, and hocus-pocuses
were banned as unholy forms of competition.
"The divil," he'd say, then something Latin
the townspeople took to mean "anathema,"
whenever the tinkers turned up in their wagons
full of charms and spells and red-haired daughters
telling fortunes and selling talismans.
Argyle got there quite by accident—
a wrong turn on the coastal road en route
to Loop Head where a sinner lay stone-dead
by dint of the eighty-some-odd years he'd lived
on that peninsula. But when the priest got wind
of it, he sent his acolytes to bring
the sin-eater in for inquisitioning.
And Argyle humored him all night until
the priest made threats of holy violence,
to which Argyle, grinning, said, "Good priest, relent.
You do a brisk trade in indulgences
and tithes and votive lamps and requiems.
You keep your pope and robes and host and chalice.
Leave me my loaf and bowl and taste for malice."

ARGYLE'S RETURN TO THE HOLY ISLAND

After the dream of the church dove and the tongues,
Argyle contemplated pilgrimage
to that blessed island in the Hebrides
from which his ancient lineage had sprung
from the sainted loinage of Columbans
whose couplings with the island women left
a legacy of zealotry, God-hunger,
genius, and the occasional idiot
that worked its way down blighted centuries
of monks and anchorites and sin-eaters—
a race of men much gifted with their mouths
for giving out with prayers and poetry
or, like Argyle, for the eating of
sinful excess, shortfalls, mediocrities,
such as would set most lesser men to vomiting.
With neither mule nor map, Argyle walked
aimlessly throughout the western places
until he came to water, which he crossed
from island to smaller island praising
the fierce weather, the full moon, the faithful boatmen.
What makes this aching in the soul? he thought,
for distant islands where the silence hoards
the voices of our dead among the stones?
And though no answer was forthcoming he went forth.

ARGYLE'S STONE

Around his neck Argyle wore a stone:
green marble from the strand at Iona
where Columcille and his banished kinsmen
landed after bloody Cooldrevny claimed
three thousand in 561 AD.
"To every cow its calf; to books their copy!"—
the notion that begat that savagery.
His ruminations on such histories
put him in mind of how most mortals kept
committing the same sin over and over
like calving cows or Psalter manuscripts—
each a version of the original.
Among his pendant stone's known properties:
general healing, protection from fire,
shipwreck, miscarriage, and other dire
possibilities that might imperil
a pilgrim of Argyle's appetites.
Foremost among the sin-eater's lapses
were hunger, which was constant, and then thirst,
and all known iterations of desire—
craving and coveting, lusting and glut:
whatever was was never quite enough.
So for ballast among such gravities
Argyle wore the stone; for anchorage.

ARGYLE AT LOOP HEAD

Argyle kept to the outposts and edges,
cliff rocks, coastal roads, estuary banks,
sheltering in dry ditches, thick hedges,
forts and cabin ruins, beside stone ranks,
much scorned by men, much put-upon by weather.
The weeping of keeners brought him hither,
fresh grief, fresh graves, lights in dark localities—
such signs and wonders of mortality
drew him toward the living and the dead
to foment pardon in a bowl of beer
or leaven remission out of common bread,
and when his feast was finished disappear.
The bodies of the dead he dined over
never troubled Argyle but still
their souls went with him into exile
and, reincarnate as gulls and plovers,
dove from high headlands over the ocean
in fits of hopeful flight, much as heaven
was said to require a leap of faith
into the fathomless and unbeknownst.
Sometimes the urge to follow them was so
near overwhelming he could almost taste
the loss of gravity in brackish air,
his leap, the sea's embrace, his savior.

ARGYLE'S EUCHARIST

Upright over corpses it occurred to him—
the body outstretched on a pair of planks,
the measly loaf and stingy goblet,
the gobsmacked locals, their begrudging thanks,
the kinswomen rummaging for coppers—
it came into his brain like candlelight:
his lot in life like priesthood after all.
Such consolations as the kind he proffered,
by sup and gulp consuming mortals' sins,
quenching hellfire, dousing purgatory,
transforming requiems to baptismals;
but for holy orders and a church,
bells and vestments and lectionary,
a bishop, benefice, or sinecure,
the miracles were more or less the same:
a transubstantiation, sleight and feint,
a reconfiguration of accounts
whereby he took unto himself the woe
that ought betide the rotting decadent.
Perdition due the recent decedent
thus averted by Argyle's hunger,
the unencumbered soul makes safe to God,
the decomposing dead get buried under
earth and stone. The sin-eater belches, wipes his gob.

A CORPORAL WORK OF MERCY

"God bless all here, the living and the dead!"
Thus spake Argyle ducking through the door.
A woman's corpse outstretched on the stone floor
was yellow jaundiced and so corpulent
the wizened man hunched sobbing next to it
in deep paroxysms of grief and shame
could neither hoist her on the table nor
drag the fat cadaver from the place.
So setting candles at her head and feet
he'd kept the vigil raising his lament
while praying for sufficient aid to move her
before he was evicted by the stench.
Argyle, moved by such entreaties, bent
such powers as he had to the removal,
taking up those huge shanks by the ankles
he hauled away and the husband pushed her.
After half a morning's massive labors
they'd got her out the back door to the haggard—
a heap among the spuds and cabbages
of putrefaction and composting grief—
and knowing that the job was incomplete
they set to work with spades and dug a ditch
of such surpassing depth and length and breadth. . .
it was after dark they shoved her into it.

ARGYLE CONSIDERS THE ELEMENTS

Argyle surveyed the ominous maw
of tempest assembling off Kilbaha
in the pike's Mouth of the River Shannon,
obscuring the white strand at Ballybunion
and County Kerry's western expanses:
the lay of the land in all directions
blackened with calamity's sure advance.
The sin-eater, given to introspection,
wondered was it something he ate or drank
over the gray corpse of a publican
the night before in Kilballyowen.
Possibly, a sinfulness so grotesque
even his scapegoating could not redress it
and so the heavens would themselves exact
prompt compensation through an Act of God:
whirlwind, maelstrom, lightning and thunderclap,
fissure or freak wave, black frost or flash-flood—
he'd seen this balancing of books before.
The bishop of Galway was swallowed whole,
swept off the planet by a cataract
and gobbled up by the sea's upheaval—
something to do with a woman and her boy
against whose innocence he had inveighed.
No glimpse of him was ever got again.

ARGYLE AMONG THE MOVEEN LADS

The Moveen lads were opening a grave
in Moyarta, for Porrig O'Loinsigh,
got dead in his cow cabin in between two
Friesans, their udders bursting, his face gone blue.
"As good a way to go as any, faith,"
said Canon McMahon the parish priest
"Sure, wasn't our savior born in such a place?"
Unmoved by which rhetorical, the lads
kept mum but for their picks and spades which rang
out their keen begrudgeries and gratitudes.
"God spare the labor and the laborers!"
So quoth Argyle, passing in the road.
"The last among the earthen decencies—
this shovel and shoulder work by which are borne
our fellow pilgrims on their journeys home."
Uplifted by which utterance, the lads
proffered whiskey, gobeens of local cheese,
a cut of plug tobacco. "Take your ease
with us awhile," said one, "here among the bones
of the dead man's elders buried years ago,
now resurrected by our excavations."
And there among old stones his contemplations
hovered among femurs and holding up a skull,
"Alas," he said, "O'Loinsigh, I knew him well!"

HIS AMBULATIONS

On shank's mare Argyle talked to himself.
Alone, he'd carry on whole colloquies
en route to some poor corpse's obsequies—
these dialogues, the way he kept his wits
about him, body and soul together,
fit for the wretched work of sin-eating.
Sometimes he counted words or parts of words
as if they amounted to something more
than sound and sense attuned between his ears,
as, for example, how coincident:
the way *grace* and *gratis*, wherefore *gratitude*
partook a kinship such as cousins do,
singing the same tune in different voices,
much as *grave* and *gravitas*, then *gravity*
kept one earthbound, grounded, humble as the mud—
the *humus*, so called, God wrought *humans* from.
Or how from Adam's rib was fashioned Eve—
bone of his own bone, flesh of his flesh—
whom he got *gravid* by implanting seed,
in her unfathomably fecund Eden.
The memory of a woman's company
would bring his ambulations to a halt
to aim his gaping face due heavenward,
the dewy air her touch; her taste, sweet salt.

HIS REPASTS

He ate the boiled breakfast and the fry—
rashers and puddings, eggs and porridge oats,
late tea with milk and sugar, every night
he could get it, some nights a lump of goat
cheese or sausage with it. Such were his habits.
As for the dinner, long accreted sins
served up with corpses and a gainful wage
(in keeping with his station and remit)
were all that ever really satisfied.
Tough work, alas, still someone had to do it.
No less the mutes and watchers, wailing hags,
who kept their vigils at all local wakes
beating their breasts, enacting pantomimes,
waiting to see in case the dead would rise
to the occasion: spirits and soul cakes.
Whereupon the reverend curate's narrative
of how the poor cratur was yet alive
and writhing no doubt in purgatory
would haunt the living through the dark of night.
Mid-morning's when Argyle would arrive
and for a fraction of the churchman's fee,
he'd tender sweet remission, clean the plate
of every crumb and drain the tankard.
The dead, thus left to their contingencies,
the living carried on their theaters.

HE CONSIDERS NOT THE LILIES BUT THEIR EXCELLENCIES

Thin gruel, shallow graves, whiskey watered down,
the ne'er-do-well and good-for-nothing crowd
of cornerboys and gobshites were among
Argyle's manifold perturbations.
Worse still, the episcopal vexations:
their excellencies, eminences, and graces,
red cassocked dandies and mitered wankers,
the croziered posers in their bishoprics
with their Easter duties and Peter's pence,
their ledgers full of mortal, venial sins—
keepers of the till and tally, bankers
of indulgences and dispensations;
their bulls and bans and excommunications,
nothing but contumely and bamboozles.
For all their vestiture, rings, and unctions,
preaching to bishops, like farting at skunks, was
nothing but a mug's game to the sin-eater,
so in earshot of them mum is what he kept.
Still, he thought there might be something to it:
a life apart from this life where the souls
long dead and gone were neither dead nor gone.
Some days he felt so happily haunted,
by loving ghosts and gods upholding him.
Some days he felt entirely alone.

HE WEEPS AMONG THE CLARE ANTIQUITIES

At Poulnabrone Dolmen Argyle poured
his soul's ache into the hole of sorrows,
huddling under the ancient capstone
against the cold and crueler elements.
Stone portal, stone cairn, stone everywhere—
the rocky desert of the Burren bore
a semblance to his own hard-weathered heart
made barren by years of cast aspersions, pox,
maledictions, cursed loneliness and loss.
Only by wretching over the earth's bone box,
or pissing on the effigy at Corcomroe,
or making for the graveyard at Fanore
to visit his late, great confessor's tomb—
(the druid holy man O'Donahue's)—
could he purge himself of bile and rancor
so, this twice or thrice a yearly pilgrimage
up the West Clare coast and down again
lightened the load of comeuppance his grim
work among the newly dead occasioned.
Among old stones a calm came over him
as if the dead beneath them held their own
redemptions on their journeys heavenward,
like wildflowers gathered out of bones,
their sweet bouquets a comfort beyond words.

ARGYLE AT THE ENNIS FRIARY

Among the friars minor Argyle
kept his silence and meditations on
the joyous and sorrowful mysteries,
and dwelt on Transitus—the holy soul's
last pilgrimage—in imitation of
the saint's embrace of Sister Death in Assisi
the third of October 1226.
Argyle prayed to purge his dreams of sex
with minoresses in their brown habits,
busy at their blessedness, their sweet breasts
swelling under scapulars, their fine hands
always at the work of heaven, their hush
a constant prayer for continence of flesh,
as Poor Clare's order had accustomed them
to poverty, chastity, obedience.
God help Argyle, he could not help himself:
for all his pieties and flagellations,
the taste of Sister Mary on his tongue,
the touch of her fingers on his person,
the safe hold and harbor of her body
became the icons of his supplications;
to lie as Francis had, naked and alone,
just once before the end, and to show her
the love of God such as he'd come to know it.

HE POSITS CERTAIN MYSTERIES

The body of the boy who took his flight
off the cliff at Kilcloher into the sea
was hauled up by curragh-men, out at first light
fishing mackerel in the estuary.
"No requiem or rosary," said the priest,
"nor consecrated ground for burial,"
as if the boy had flown outside the pale
of mercy or redemption or God's love.
"Forgive them, for they know not what they do,"
quoth Argyle to the corpse's people,
who heard in what he said a sort of riddle,
as if he meant their coreligionists
and not their sodden, sadly broken boy.
Either way, they took some comfort in it
and readied better than accustomed fare
of food and spirits; by their own reckoning:
the greater sin, the greater so the toll.
But Argyle refused their shilling coin
and helped them build a box and dig a grave.
"Your boy's no profligate or prodigal,"
he said, "only a wounded pilgrim like us all.
What say his leaping was a leap of faith,
into his Father's beckoning embrace?"
They killed no fatted calf. They filled the hole.

HIS PURGATIONS

Argyle shat himself and, truth be told,
but for the mess of it, the purging was
no bad thing for the body corporal.
Would that the soul were so thoroughly cleansed,
by squatting and grunting supplications.
Would that purgatories and damnations
could be so quickly doused and recompensed,
null and voided in the name of mercy.
He made for Goleen and a proper laving
of his crotch and loins and paltry raiments.
Outstretched on the strand, his body's immersion
in the tide was not unlike a christening:
two goats for godparents, two herring gulls
perched in the current his blessed parents,
a fat black cormorant the parish priest
anointing him with chrisms and oils,
pronouncing him reborn, renamed, renewed
in the living waters of baptism.
In every dream he dreamt after bathing,
the guilt and guile of his sin-eating
and all accrued perditions were absolved
and he was named after an apostle
or martyr or evangelist or saint,
welcome everywhere, forgiven everything.

ARGYLE ON KNOCKNAGAROON

Because he barely heard the voice of God
above the tune of other choristers—
batwing and bird-whistle, gathering thunder,
the hiss of tides retreating, children, cattle—
because he could not readily discern
the plan Whoever Is in Charge Here has,
he wondered about those who claimed to have
blessed assurances or certainty:
a One and Only Way and Truth and Life,
as if Whatever Breathes in Everything
mightn't speak in every wondrous tongue;
as if, of all creations, only one
made any sense. It made no sense to him.
Hunger he understood, touch, desire.
He knew the tenderness humans could do,
no less brutalities. He knew the cold
morning, the broad meadow, the gold sunset.
One evening on the hill of Knocknagaroon,
the Atlantic on one side, the Shannon
on the other, the narrowing headlands
of the peninsula out behind him,
the broad green palm of Moveen before him,
it seemed he occupied the hand of God:
open, upturned, outstretched, uplifting him.

RECOMPENSE HIS PARACLETE

His paraclete was a piebald donkey
bequeathed him by a sad-eyed parish priest
whose sins he supped away one Whitsunday
some months in advance of your man's demise.
"Never a shortage of asses, Argyle,
   God knows we've all got one of them at least."
Which truth seemed surplus to requirements.
Argyle named the wee jack Recompense
and got good orderly direction from it.
Wherever the one went, so went the other
bearing mighty nature's burdens wordlessly,
the brown sign of the cross across their backs.
The last was ever seen of them was headed west—
a tatterdemalion and his factotum—
making for the coast road in the cold and gloaming,
braying and flailing out gestures of blessing
over hedgerow and hay bales, man and beast
alike, hovel and out-office, dung heap and home,
everything in eye and earshot rectified:
cats pardoned, curs absolved, tethered cattle loosed,
and all of vast creation reconciled
in one last spasm of forgiveness.
As for the sin-eater and Recompense,
where the road turned toward the sea they turned with it.

CLOUD OF WITNESSES: NEW POEMS

A LAVING SONG

By water and the ancient codes we claim
this wriggling child for our kind and tribe
and call down blessings in the Blessed Name
of Nature and Creation, praying, "God,
God, safeguard this human against all evils.
Save him from cruel happenstance and cold.
Let him outlive us by a hundred years,
awash in grace, made fierce by faith, grown old
and wise, free of our most grievous foibles.
Today we proclaim he is one of ours,
with chrisms and singing, candles aflame
with Pentecostal tongues and paschal light
by which we reckon he will find his way
back home to you in the fullness of time.
And so we hold him up to heaven's face
(See how he reaches for the bright abyss!)
so You will recognize one of Your own,
and know his voice when he cries out to You
as he most surely will; as we all do.
We call upon his cloud of witnesses—
our ancients and elders and our long lost—
to breathe into him all the holy ghosts
by whom we are well haunted and still blessed
and beckoned to what is or isn't next.

LIBRA

The one who pulled the trigger with his toe,
spread-eagled on his girlfriend's parents' bed,
and split his face in halves above his nose,
so that one eye looked east, the other west;

sometimes that sad boy's bifurcation seems
to replicate the math of love and grief—
that zero sum of holding on and letting go
by which we split the differences with those

with whom we occupy the present moment.
Sometimes I see that poor corpse as a token
of doubt's sure twin and double-mindedness,
of certainty, the countervailing guess,

the swithering, the dither, righteousness,
like Libra's starry arms outstretched in love
or supplication or, at last, surrender
to the scales forever tipped in the cold sky.

ACCORDION

We'd been invited to a
neighborhood do:
a graduation maybe,
or a barbecue.
We were underdressed,
the missus and me,
but I had my accordion
which is, unfailingly,
a compensation.
Whatever happened
there was this chute—
like the slides
we played on
in our childhoods.
It ascended
from the center of
the neighbors' yard
into the heavens
beyond the sky
like a spiral staircase
without the steps.
And it came into my brain
they'd like to hear something
from the topmost
heights of it. So
I began to climb
on all fours
with the accordion
on my back
wheezing out the
occasional chord,
myself huffing

and puffing with the
baffling labor of it;
my wife's sweet face
gaping heavenward,
the locals wide-eyed
with the spectacle. Everything
was shaky at the top
which I accomplished.
I know that for sure.
Though I can't for the
life of me remember
what number I played them,
or the applause that
would have just as
certainly followed.
We were fairly winded,
the accordion and I,
what with the whole performance.

YOU WHO NEVER CAME IN

after Rilke

You who never came in
to my embrace, oh my heart, ever distant
by design, here's another tune
there is no telling
whether you'll approve. I've quit
trying to discern your
part in everything that happens. The things I've seen,
all that I've imagined: far cities,
oceans, islands, evenings, esplanades,
the heaving, tidal pulses of creation
that always seem to signal
you, just beyond my touch, my hold.

You, beloved, who are all the old
dreams I've ever wakened from,
wanting: a cottage door
swung open to the weather, and you
at the window looking out. Or
turning a corner, lost in thought, out ahead of me, gone again.
Or in the glass of passing traffic, the endless transit, a glance
of you and then of me, alone at the curb. Who knows? Maybe
that rain this morning fell on the two of us, our dewy, separate,
upturned faces, glistening.

NATIVITY

Some years the sky falls harder than others.
The great go hush, good neighbors, poets, priests—
woe's dreadful litany knows no surcease.
The dead are everywhere, and there's the bother.
Miserere nobis, Lord, dust to dust
is pity little in the way of solace.
Our shaken sense of what comes next leaves us,
like as not, disconsolate. Unless
we count them in our cloud of witnesses,
their voices rising like a distant chorus,
tunes we always knew or thought we knew,
much as the multitude of the heavenly host
sang to shepherds attending their sheep
anthems of joy and peace, praise and glory.
Said one to the others, "Let us go and see,"
in Luke's much told version of the story.
And so, emboldened by what the angel told them,
off they went toward Bethlehem to find
the swaddled babe and manger and lolling beasts,
their beauty and their beings ramified
in carols lightening our lamentations;
and held aloft, somehow, the starry skies.

YOSSEF

Some days I wake up angry at everything—
the dreams, the voices, the cross-backed donkey,
the bulging, gravid girl, the cuckoldry,
the troth I pledged regardless: love's a yoke.
Life's a gibbet, time's a torment and a thorn:
I am an old man, and she is beautiful.
These dark-of-night, footsore, long-haul journeys:
the occupier's tally and tax, this
murderous fiat. I'm too old for this.
I've got better things to do. To build,
to join. I make do, shelter, and husband.
Give her her due, the child's a bright star—
graceful like her, her calm, those wellspring eyes.
The herdsmen were dumbstruck, the Levantines—
their camels and wariness. Perfumes and gold?
What's frankincense and myrrh to refugees?
Our lot's a scourge, the way a mystery.
Some days it's magic just to be alive.

SOME OCTAVES ON HOLY ORDERS

A vestibule bathed in stained-glass light
for naming and claiming, chrism and oil.
The fidgeting novices swaddled in white,
laved and anointed, joyously hoist up
heavenward, buried with the crucified.
The blood-proud elders, all kinship and foibles,
I loved those Saturdays with dads and moms,
the bracing splash in the baptismal font.

Binding and loosing was frightening business:
the fear of perdition and comeuppance—
the jot and tittle of guilt and contrition,
the shalt and thou shalt not accountancy
of holding on and letting go, remission
of sins in trade for true repentances.
Bless me Father for I have sinned, they'd plead.
I'd give out Hail Mary's and Glory Be's.

That *hoc est corpus* with the loaf and cup—
the body and blood work of sacrifice—
a transubstantiation, bit and sup,
table and blade replaced by host and chalice;
the fervent with their open palms and mugs,
after Melchizedek's ancient praxis,
the endless, famished line of them—vapors
of a life's long work and love's hard labor.

Every year the archbishop visits
to have a look around and count receipts,
to tap the faces of brothers and sisters,
their flaming ureai, their Paraclete
hissing above, gifts of tongues and spirits,
this laying on of hands, a bloom, replete:
much like the descent of the holy ghost
on frightened disciples, gobsmacked and aghast.

I might have married. I know about love:
the heart's privations, the body's urgency.
For years I ached but offered it all up
for suffering souls and prayed for constancy.
The calling I got was the faintest summons,
an intimation only, a sense of things,
a soul ramifying and forever
silent, beyond silence listened for.

The blessed sacrament: viaticum—
a toll for the boatmen at the crossing,
a balm for the road home, an extreme unction
against the shaken faith, the getting lost.
Last rites, last words, the *lacrimae rerum*:
the way their old eyes reddened at the blessing—
my thumb tracing crosses with the unguent—
makes me think there must be something to it.

In Romans, chapter one, verse twenty-five,
Paul claims mistaking creatures for creator
is much the same as trading truth for lies,
as if the made thing were itself the maker.
Yeats wrestled with such curiosities
in that poem: *great-rooted blossomer. . .*
O body swayed to music, O brightening glance,
How can we know the dancer from the dance?

And after fifty years, they look the same:
the thing itself, the idea of the thing,
the ancients and the infants, sinners, saints,
all fellow pilgrims, saved and suffering,
the passion and the passionate, the same
but different. Wherefore my surety:
The way and truth and life? Our holy orders?
The bottom line? God's love. Love one another.

WHEN SHE KNEW

The way her lover peeled the sunburned flesh
From her reddened shoulder, then kissed the place
And ate the desiccated tissue of her
Like any succulent, was when she knew

The hunger of bodies for other bodies,
The intimate succor and comfort between
Wounds and private parts and secret spaces
And how one opens to another's touch.

RECOMPENSE

That year they kept the usual routines:
aubade and evensong, the world's sad news,
the work, the house and grounds, the annual dues;
they fed the animals, studied stars for signs,
ate right, slept soundly, hoisted cups half full,
counted their blessings, kept no count of hurts,
and strove, in all aspects, to be grateful,
sensible, upright, salutary sorts.

Alas, in spite of it, their hearts were broken
often as not by those beloved of them—
the ones who died, the ones who, not yet gone,
were distanced, embittered, better left alone.

But Hark! For all such losses were restored
when Lo! Behold! To them a child was born.

HOW HOWARD ARMSTRONG LEARNED
THE VERITIES

Because he made a prayer of everything,
his labor, rest, and play were much the same—
offered up to God in thanksgiving
for the day that was in it, and its grace.
Because his father kept the names and dates
of who got buried when and where and such
Howard Armstrong used to open graves
in West Highland, then he'd close them up:
a manful job he did for twenty bucks,
twenty-five in the winters once the frost
hold tightened in the topsoil. He kept
a fire underneath an upturned cattle trough
which fit the space he needed near enough,
smoldering all night on scrap-wood and tires,
by daybreak the topsoil loosened up
so that a couple hours' shovel work
through mud and clay and stones and he'd be done;
he'd swing a pick to square the corners off.
And this is how he learned the verities,
last things and corporal works of mercy;
how every man's appointed once to die:
earth to earth, ashes to ashes, dust, dust,
and everyone among us needs someone
to open ground or tend a fire at the end,
to get our bodies where they need to go,
and pray the pilgrim soul safe home again.

THE DESERT YEARS

Such evil as the evil that we prayed
Befall their people had befallen ours
As if we'd mouthed our curses in a mirror:
Blight them, O Lord, and were thereby blighted.
As if we were our own worst enemies—
Our bridges burned, our boundless enmity
Turned back on us though God was on our side.

AT MOYARTA

a burial in West Clare

So, here's Maura Carmody,
Late of Moveen West, Kilkee,
Who, last Sunday after Mass,
Couldn't catch her breath, alas!

Thence to Limerick Hospital
Where the meds did not avail.
Monday she gave up the ghost,
Gone to ground, to God we hope.

Left to mourn, her family
Proffers these sad obsequies.
Open earth, please take her back;
God keep Maura if we can't.

TWELVE DAYS OF CHRISTMAS

Some pilgrims claim the carol is a code
for true believers and their catechists,
to wit: four colly birds, four gospel texts,
eight maids a-milking, the beatitudes,
and pipers piping, the eleven left
once Judas had betrayed the lamb of God—
that partridge in a pear tree, the holy one
and only whose nativity becomes
in just a dozen days the starlit eve
of three french hens with their epiphanies
huddled round the family in the manger,
tendering their gold and frankincense and myrrh.
The whole tune seems to turn on "five golden rings"—
the Pentateuch, those first books of the Torah
in which ten lords a-leaping stand in for
the ten commandments cut in loaves of stone
which Moses broke over his wayward tribesmen.
Two turtle doves, two testaments, old and new.
Six geese a laying, creation's shortened week,
the swimming swans, gifts of the Holy Ghost
whose fruits become withal nine ladies dancing.
Twelve drummers drumming, the Apostles' Creed:
a dozen doctrines to profess belief in.
Still, others say it's only meant to praise
fine feathered birds and characters and rings,
our singing nothing more than thanksgiving
for litanies of underserved grace,
unnumbered blessings, the light's increasing,
our brightly festooned trees bedazzling.

WHAT SHALL WE SAY?

A triptych for Thomas G. Long:
teacher, preacher, presbyter

I.

The etymology is perilous:
pulpit from *pulpitum*, meaning "*scaffold*,"
by which we come, at length, to *catafalque*—
those *f*'s and *a*'s, like tongue-and-grooved boards,
like rope enough to hang, or hoist, or let
a corpse down to its permanent repose.
One platform's raised; one frames a coffin's rest.
So, first the elocution, then the wake?
Like lamentations or the case of Job—
that vexing, god-awful, comfortless book.
And yet we rise to the occasion,
Sunday after Sunday after Sunday.
A bit of scripture, a psalm or poem,
something that happened in the week just past;
we try to weave them all together as
if to say a loving God's in charge.
As if we were certain of a loving God.
We see by faith. We live in hope. We love.
Or play the odds, as Pascal did. We fall.
Sometimes it all seems quite impossible.
And yet we rise again and walk the plank,
and sing into oblivion good news:
Unto God the glory, all praise, all thanks!
while nodding congregants loll in their pews.

II.

Imagine Tom out on the fire escape,
between the world at large and inner life,
edging the proscenium, downstage right,
whilst curios and characters and shades

unveil themselves as dancing beauties do.
I have tricks in my pocket, things up my sleeve!
Upstage, sheer curtains rise, transparencies:
Truth in the pleasant guise of illusion.

Like John on Patmos, John the Harbinger—
voices crying out of the wilderness—
Make straight ye the Lord's way! quoth Isaiah.
Eschatology and Apocalypse:

Think Esmeralda in the cathedral,
Jim Hawkins in the riggings, chased by Hands
or Ishmael, just flotsam at the end,
alone, before God and all these people.

Or Montaigne in his tower library:
"the whole of Man's estate in every man."
Or Yeats pacing the boards at Ballylee:
"How can we know the dancer from the dance?"

Thus, exegetes and preachers on their own
hold forth, against a never-ceasing din
of second-guessing, out there on their limbs:
Have faith! Behold, the mystery! Behold!

III.

That fresco of the *Sermon on the Mount*
by Fra Angelico (dear brother John)
shows Jesus semicircled by his men,
gilt-haloed Galileans but for one,
who will betray him later with a kiss,
atop their sandstone tuffets, rapt, engaged.
He's going on about beatitudes,
fulfillments of the law, the words to pray.
Outside the frame, unseen, a multitude
leans in to listen to the hermeneutics,
which are not without some challenges, to wit:
though we be smitten, turn the other cheek,
go the second mile, love our enemies;
while we're forgiven only so much as
we forgive those who trespass against us.
A certain eye-for-eyeness to that scheme,
a tooth-for-toothedness. A quid pro quo?
As if, to finally get, we must let go?
Sometimes it's so, sometimes it isn't? So,
what shall we say to these things? Who's to know?
Say who abides in love abides in God.
Say God is love. Love God. Love one another.
Say grace is undeserved and plentiful.
Say if we're saved, it's mostly from ourselves.

RECEIPT

for Christopher Reid

Typeset in ten-point Requiem your brief
blue file, *Anniversary*, arrived.
Oh Chris! Ten years since your Lucinda died?
We never feel the time, the rounding sweep,
it makes of everything; its *clearances*
to use the word that Heaney used for when
we get the grain and hammer angled right:
the split, the cut, the coal block and the stone
cold fact of life, the fact of death, we die.
These strike it rich, these *in memoriam*s.

ST. KEVIN AND THE TEMPTRESS

after Heaney

After that business with the blackbird, Kevin
sore-shouldered from his mortifications—
the lent-long arms reach and supplications

in service of life's mysteries and flights—
lay himself out, spread-eagled in paschal light,
cozy in a copse of alders, cones, and catkins,

and slept the sleep of a child of God.
Waking to a woman fast astraddle him
in ways he'd never ere experienced

and sensing frenzy in his nether regions
so lovely that it must be mortal sin,
he strove against the ginger-haired Kathleen

pressing her pudenda against his parts
whilst writhing midst her own deliriums,
the palms of her small hands warm to his heart,

like riding the tide of Love's deep river,
groaning approval and grateful *te deum*s—
a prayer her being made entirely.

Whereupon the monk woke to his senses
and grabbing the temptress by her attributes,
in righteous warp-spasms of rectitude,

tackled her into the lough's chill waters,
the better to chasten, he thought, brute nature,
mighty as it was, please God; and that was that.

PERSONAL

Am old and fat and bald and married (twice).
Don't drink, don't smoke; I piss and moan too much.
I fart and snore but otherwise am nice
enough. And though I amn't rich, I want
for nothing. Some say I'm generous
to a fault. Others, that I'm too forgiving.
Am looking for someone to travel with
to Ireland, early on next year.
I've a small place on the coast of West Clare
between Kilkee and Loop Head. Check the map.
It's a lovely, wild, treeless country
between the ocean and the estuary.
Great sunsets, cliff walks by the sea, wildflowers,
rainbows, rolling meadows. You can Google it.
The little bookish festivals are fun—
the nights infused with merriment and song.
Maybe you'd rather talks by the fire?
Twisting relations with the broguey neighbors?
Suit yourself. You could plan to sleep alone.
I'm only after good conversation,
someone to share the mealtimes with, the road,
the eventual sadness of it all.
I'm so tired of talking to myself.
I want to hear a voice that isn't mine,
maybe ask how the day went, would I like
a sup of decaf, a lump of goat cheese?
I don't know. No hard-and-fast requirements;
no romance, no swooning, no bungee-jumping, just
ordinary talk. No feigned climaxes,
no breathless afterglow, just some chitchat
and commiseration for a month or so.
I lift the seat, wipe things clean, put it down again.

HER MOTHER'S IRISES

No ideas but in things, I tell her
Dr. Williams tells us in a poem.
Say it: this is just to say those plums
in the fridge, a red wheelbarrow
upon which so much does, indeed, depend—
the glaze of rainwater, the white chickens—
confer, in their bland thingy-ness a key,
a cypher for the mystery of things.
And here's something: she walks out to the sea,
returning with the wildflowers picked
on the anniversary of her mother's death
now sixteen Junes ago, and how her father kept
a paper bag full of dusty tubers
saved for his daughter—small consolations:
her mother's irises—now grown beyond her care.
It's a thing with her, she sows them everywhere.

SAN CASSIANO

for Dualco De Dona and Francesco Paladini, il dottore

St. Cassian of Imola refused
all sacrifices to the gods of Rome,
pagan as they seemed to him, so, true to form,
the emperor ordered him executed.
It was Julian the Apostate
who gave the teacher over to his students
because they bore abundant grudgeries
for the rigors of the saint's strict tutelage.
What little of his story still known
involves the stake they bound him to, the slow
torment of their styli incising him,
as if his flesh were wax on which to grave
the saga of his grisly martyrdom,
the thirteenth of August 363,
which became, wherefore, his official feast.
Some centuries after that they built a church
and christened a square for him in Venice,
commissioned paintings by Tintoretto—
The Crucifixion, The Risen Christ with Saints,
The Descent of Jesus into Limbo—
postcards of which are offered now for sale,
to faithful and apostate, one and all.
I paid the toll and lit a candle there
and sent a card that read *Wish you were here.*

PAR RUM PUM PUM PUM

> *The ox knoweth his owner, and the ass his master's crib...*
> —Isaiah 1:3

The Holy Father, in a recent book
on the infancy of Jesus, Christ the Lord,
banished the angels always heard on high
and lowing beasts from the Nativity,
those manger scenes and crèches notwithstanding,
the figurines of lowly animals,
their steamy exhalations warming the babe,
more myth, so says the pope, than scriptural.
My jackass, Charles, has begun to mope
around the haggard, inconsolable
as that giant Canaanite and erstwhile saint
who shouldered Christ across the river once,
downsized, alas, to "Mister" Christopher
by another pope, who some few years ago
consigned him to the hinterlands of faith.
As for Charles, my gelded, piebald ass,
he's borne such burdens as were his to bear,
on Sundays carting Christians off to Mass
much as a forebearer bore Mary hence,
fat, gravid with God's Lamb to Bethlehem,
same as the magi and their camels came
laden with homage and epiphany,
their way lit by a guiding star's bright light,
now dimmed some by the magisterium.
The time I've spent with asses was well spent
and taught me reticence, humility,
and reverence for their mighty natures;
whereas my time with hierarchs has wrought
little but wariness at the ways of men

who claim to have such eminence and grace
and proud dominion over lesser beings
for which the heart marks time: *par rum pum pum pum.*

WATERFOWL AT SUMMER'S END

The gull perched on the boat hoist canopy
could be my father or my mother, both long gone,
incarnates from that cloud of witnesses
by whom we all are so happily haunted.
It is autumn; the air is gray with ghosts.
The loon that has for days and nights kept float
its vigil in the shallows, yodeling
its loneliness and warning—might it be
the remnant of my friend the parish priest
whose heart gave out last year, so suddenly—
a holy man who wore his holiness
like an old coat always shared with others?
And Norm, our Norm could be that cormorant
making its way north against the headwinds,
as if the winter weren't coming next,
and the cold and the frost hold and the snow.
Has he some message meant for us? Who knows?
What if the mute swans in the river's mouth
are Dennis, dead some Christmases ago,
and Seamus, his eulogist, his hero, gone
to ground in South Derry, the sycamores,
the clutch of earth around them tightening?
What if they occupy a bright nowhere,
so blinding in its luminosity,
so far beyond our reckonings we dare
not hope, but only wonder what we see?

MOVEEN SOLSTICE

Bees abound in the *Rosa rugosa*,
Wildly overgrown, the *Olearia*
Wants cutting back, the haggards mowing.
The whitethorn hedge and alder should be pruned,
The chimney swept, cow-cabins shoveled out,
And doors left open because it's June
And the sweet breath of Cuba in the air
Has made its ocean crossing finally
In counterclockwise northeast orbitings
To wash ashore a few fields north of here
Its warm anointing inundating
Through gaps and gates, cross ditches, over walls
Among springers and weanlings, mares and foals,
Shorthorns, Friesians, Charolais, Belgian blues,
Whilst J.J. and Sonny talk silage and prices,
The shape of the weather, and Michael is
Whitewashing the garden wall and Maura,
Golden in late light, brings the dry linens in.

FLOTILLA

Not the designer couples with cocktails,
and downstate neighbors idling by
on pontoon barges, all sunscreen and gossip,

nor the flat-decked bass boats with sportsmen casting
crankbaits and faux worms into the shallows,
or kayakers paddling amiably by,

but that old guy in his twelve-foot aluminum,
with his dad's tackle box and rattling Evinrude,
the mutt and the missus and the secret spot

for lake perch, maybe a pike or walleye.
I envy him the most, his vintage wiles,
their colloquies, those steadfast silences,

the good drift that brings them, rain or shine,
nowhere in particular, in cahoots,
both eager to go along for the ride.

GENESIS 3

In Defendante Ferrari's panel of
Eve Tempted by the Serpent only a
filigree leaf frond from a sapling tree
tastefully obscures her mons veneris.
For the moment she is still ignorant,
not yet embarrassed by her nakedness—
how God, mannish in His heaven, fashioned her.
Later she'll get blamed for everything,
her comeliness and breasts that in this painting are
those of a fourteen- or fifteen-year-old
will become sources of sweetness and of guilt.
The serpent's head is an old bearded man
leering at her, all lechery. "Yes, yes,"
it must be hissing as she bends the branch
and reaching upward with her perfect hand
takes hold of the fruit of the Tree of Knowledge.
This is the last hour of Paradise,
the girl and her consort oblivious to
good and evil and their ramifications,
Their bites of the tree's fruit not yet taken.
The fig leaves are only fig leaves;
their genitalia not yet shameful,
the Creator still happy with creation.
The pendant canvas in which Adam appears
ready to give in to all temptations
has been lost, alas, to the centuries.
Nor can we know how he held her at the end,
grateful for her succor and constancy.

FRANCHISE 2016

I.

So, sixty-three percent of white men spent
their franchise on a fellow like themselves
who hadn't a chance and only ran because
the system's rigged against us; the likes of us
can't get a break, what with the immigrants,
dishonest media, and welfare cheats.
We want it back the way it was before
Fake news, the feminazis, and the queers,
Before the Kenyan anti-Christ. Eight years
Of hope and change? Enough's enough.
Eight years of step and fetching to a tune
called by a Muslim's quite enough, thank you;
what we need now's some relief, we want it told
just like it is. Enough P.C. We want a wall.
We're not about to chance it on some nasty
Woman who thinks she's smarter than us all.
Don't get us wrong, we're all for ladies, just
not this one, not now, maybe next time, maybe
not. Let's Make America Great Again.
Old white guys got us this far after all.

II.

And Christian evangelicals turned out—
Some eighty-one percent of them for Trump
because their lord and savior Jesus Christ
was crucified to save old billionaires
from political correctness, and the poor,
who should have made a seed faith offering
or said more prayers or spoke in tongues and who
ought not be given fish but taught to fish,

what's more they should be extremely vetted,
banned and banished if they're here illegally.
Did you hear the one about the two Corinthians
who walk into a bar to have a beer?
The barkeep says, We don't serve your kind here.
We only cater to real Americans,
Y'know, God fearing, good-news gospel sorts,
foot soldiers in the war on Christmas, true
believers, belongers, triumphalists,
no migrants, Mexicans, or Syrians
unless they're on the lam from Bethlehem.
God's on our side. We're wholly innocent.

III.

Some fifty-three percent of white women
cast what votes they cast for that vile man
because Benghazi or deleted emails
or else because the lesser of evils,
what makes her think a woman ever can
be leader of the free world? Get a clue.
It's better to leave well enough alone.
They all turned out to march on Washington
with sister marches all across the globe
and held their higher ground and boldly strode
to say that *women's rights were human rights*
and *Equal pay for equal work*. Some might
have wondered why we hadn't marched before;
why forty-some percent forgot to vote.
But still, I thought, we're all in this together
so donned my marching boots, dressed for the weather,
hoist up a sign that said *Come, tread with me*,
then walked the dog up Temple Road, alone.
Some women go for guys who march with them,
Still, more with those who grab them by the pussy.

CORRINE AMONG THE FRONDS OF BASIL

The leafy basil from the garden fills
the kitchen with a whiff of summer's losses
and frames the figure of a prepossessing girl
among these fronds saved from the coming frost.
She adds pine nuts and olive oil, shredded
Parmesan, fine crushed bulbs of garlic pressed
into a greeny pesto, boils pasta,
as if the sky weren't actually falling:
hell and high water in one dire week,
the bottoms falling out of everything;
two hundred thousand dead of pestilence,
my long-lost daughter, Heather, lost for keeps,
halfway through a leap year taking her leap
into the beckoning embrace of the abyss,
desperate for good riddance, cold release;
we got her home, alas, to let her go again.
And good John Lewis gone to his reward
who stood upright on Black Lives Matter Plaza,
No justice, No peace, our marching anthem,
to see him crossing Edmund Pettus Bridge,
bludgeoned, horizontal and victorious.
And word will come tonight of RBG,
notorious for justice and dissent,
equality of genders, loves and sexes,
against all poverties and contagions,
Corrine upholds these end-of-summer leaves—
with gratitude against begrudgeries.

GRATIS

This year we're just giving thanks—
a lighter lift than grudgeries,
up roofs, down chimneys, under trees—
easier to gift we think
when one size suits us all just fine,
like blessings and beatitudes.
Let us, please God, travel light,
in easy grace, free gratitude
for lengthened days, the briefer nights,
solstice and epiphanies,
a child's eyes, like stars so bright
wise magi follow, gazing.

DOUBLE SONNET FOR THE FLORIST'S SON

We both learned flora from the family business,
your greenhouses out back, our funeral homes:
birds-of-paradise and bright anthuriums,
flights of fancy through Michigan winters—
sympathies and loves, the paid respects, lost
causes, our rot and compost nature, the ghosts
and shades, the netherworlds, dank basement rooms,
root and tubers, shoot and seedling, bud and bloom,
bulbous corpses, corpus, cormus, opened ground,
the moldering succor of words; rancor and wound;
kitchen waltzes, belt buckles and whiskey breath,
grave blankets, flower beds, the boggy moss,
the papier-mâché tributes, glads and sprays of
baby's breath, carnations, daffodils and loss.

I worked the wards at the state hospital
in Pontiac to put myself through school.
We wrapped our manics, like mummies, snug and cool
in sodden sheets to induce a languor.
We fed them Thorazine and Mellaril
to keep them calm and quiet, stuporous.
I thought of you at Mercywood, the pool
on Bainbridge Island, Washington; how we're all
but flotsam in the chilly water, all
just fodder for the fire and the tomb,
just trying to make our way and keep the spark,
swimming laps and drinking juleps, getting tight.
"Deep in their roots all flowers hold the light."
Deep in repose all poets mold the dark.

INTERMENT

Possibly the earth restores
What we knew of it before
Coming to our senses when
We were born. Once gone again

Perhaps we relearn it all:
Ground sense, ceasing, all the lost
Intellections of the dust
Sciences of core and crust,

Intuitions of the dirt,
Clay and pebble, humus, loam,
Silences beyond the drone
We listened for, deeper earth's.

OLD DOGS

All smiles at May's end at the lakeside,
the lilacs and spirea newly bloomed,
the brothers are five and three and on the job
with Pop-Pop. They have their pooper-scoopers,
scouting for piles left by Bill, the dog,
for humans to step in and curse their luck:
Son of a bitch! or Shit! or What the fuck!
Can't that beast do his business in the woods?

He goes where he wants, the old man concedes.
He'll be dead in a year. Same goes for me
when the time comes. They grin, then wince, then roll their eyes.
The air astir with May and dragon flies.
Hindquarters sore, pearlescent-eyed, old Bill
barks at all that's seen and unseen, still.

THEODICY: A LAMENT

—for Dan Honan and all who helped

I thought I'd seen most everything before:
the bodies of babies on the table—
crib deaths, bad flu, some crueler happenstance,
an accident of nature or neglect,
toddlers at their tantrums, teens in car wrecks.
We'd lay them out in downsized caskets made
to fit the outsized sadness, then sort flowers.
I'd sometimes wonder, after calling hours,
exactly what had you in mind here, Lord.
Was well enough not better be left alone?
I Englished the silence much the same as Job:
Where were you, child, when I made the world?

But slaughtered school kids, teachers, first-graders?
Are we not blinded by the things we've seen?
Rent and dismembered, riddled innocents:
What shall we say to these things, Lord? Some days
we are Your chosen, others we're alone?
I'm angling for Leviathan, of course,
hoping to hook him at his riddling:
How's God all loving and all powerful
when all week long we've buried children?
Do all things work together for the good?
Dead boys and girls, ashes and dust?—Behold!
We gird our loins. The whirlwind beckons us.

And yet the blighted mothers walk upright.
Their hollowed, vacant eyes are yet afire.
And ruined fathers, harrowed, tenuous,
their slack arms, empty, open nonetheless.

And friends and neighbors, distant family,
brave the journey and god-awful quiet
to bide with them and tend the home fires.
While colleagues from their far-flung towns appear
to brace us in our desperate undertakings—
these precious, broken bodies, promises,. . .Dear
God, what good is anything in all of this?
Still, love that seems so distant seems so near.

Feast of the Epiphany 2013

THE PRINCE CONTI

They finished with the whimper, not the bang:
a "Brooklyn" and coffee at the Bombay Club,
the lazy jazz, the mahogany dark,
the leathery last of the Raj ambience,
partway in the journey, off on a lark;
the beauty of her being made him sigh.

ANOTHER MIRACLE

Schoolchildren from the Anahorish School
in green gymslips and ganseys lined the way
in honor at the churchyard in Bellaghy
sons and brother's shouldered the coffin up
toward the corner and the opened ground
beneath the sycamores, beside the brother.
I walked behind with the widow and daughter
still thinking this was all a grave mistake.
But they carried on. The priests had their say.
The piper played and then they lowered him,
much like the paralytic in Capernaum,
on ropes to be forgiven and then healed.
We all took up our mats and walked away
having never seen a thing like this before.

IN THE GENTS LOO OF THE STELLA MARIS

Armitage Shanks emblazoned on porcelain
unfailingly focused the eye of his mind
on the pissers in Pearce Fennell's Anchor Bar
in Carrigaholt, forty-some years before:
the screeching of jackdaws and hovering gulls,
the river flushing itself into the sea,
Pearce holding forth with that wary Alsatian
growling on the floor and himself in a blur
consigning the pints he was after downing
to the wall and sluice-drain and the great unseen
confluence of all things whereby everything—
Time and Life, Happenstance, Love and Memory—
all in capitals and sudden clarity
wove themselves into a manifest union
the nature of which remained just out of reach.
Possibly he had had too much to drink or
maybe the light beaming over the transom
and the day that was in it turning to gold
infused him with such permanent gratitude
that here in his sixties, sober and grinning,
what he could say is that he'd had enough,
hitch his trousers up, and make for the way home.

TO HIS GRANDCHILDREN AS
DARK DRAWS HITHER

This year I outlived your great-grandfather.
Would that he had gotten to know you all,
to hear you call "Pop-Pop," to have your small
hands grasp his fingers and lead the way
into the future you'll, please God, inhabit.
Alas, he died, as we do, as we must,
too soon; to the ones who love us, enough
will never be enough. It was September
near enough the autumnal equinox,
the equal day and equal night of things,
the season of such quiet subtractions:
green from the trees, and yes, my toddling girl,
my rollicking boys, we hardly notice
light from the days, days from the year, years from,
well, possibly in time you'll know the rest:
the heart's ineluctable arithmetic.
Sans teeth, sans eyes, sans taste, sans everything.
There are, of course, the compensations. Yes:
the leaves redden, yellow, brown, and wither
with such a fervor as could catch your breath away;
nor do they fall so much as waltz, let's say—
each in its own time, insouciant, adrift,
in languid descent, having achieved a
soft repose before they disappear
scuttling up the streets of October
to lodge among the rotting hostas,
limp ground covers, feathery evergreens,
as ye go forth, costumed, for Halloween,
Iron Man and Ninja, lemur, polar bear
out of the darkness with your bag of treats.

The week after All Souls' in November
I voted for the Methodist because
I'd heard her preach once on John Wesley's rule,
and thought it showed her heart for what it was:
broken, hopeful, beset on every side,
still more grateful than begrudging, much as mine,
despite its grievances, sometimes feels bathed in grace,
as if bereavement made us more alive
the way our elders, when they knew their ends were near,
embraced their darkness as if brightness beckoned them,
like Newgrange on the winter solstice when
sunbeams flood deep into the central chamber
and dancing ghosts and goblins on the walls
hum, it has been said, their hallelujahs
cold and broken as priestly Leonard sang them
in praise of babes in mangers, vacant tombs,
patriarchs and prophets, fruit of wombs,
paralytics who take up from their beds and walk,
remissions and forgiveness, reconcilings,
psalmists, shepherds, beasts of burden, talk
between old lovers, new ones, camels, kings
pursuing stars in search of wondrous things.
Do all the good you can, John Wesley wrote,
by any means, all ways and everywhere
whenever, whosoever, as long as ever. . .
and so our prayer for you this year: keep hope.
She lost the election but won the vote. Oh well.
The dark gives way to light another year.
So, love one another, stick together, dear
Tommy Pat, our Alexes, our bright Noelle.

PRIESTESS

Always I want to remember you, sunlit,
in Fishguard. We're dining in the golden air;
your daylong walk round the seafront roseate
in your aspect. You have braided your hair.
The sun reposing over your shoulder,
gilding twin glistening flutes of Prosecco—
one emptied, one, still sparkling, to go.
And the toothy beauty of you smiling,
smiling as if there is no tomorrow,
nor ever an instant before here and now,
seems a consecration of the elements,
an undeserved grace, the real presence.
Always I want to hold on to this moment.
Behold, my dear, the moment's hold on me.

DIGITUS PATERNAE DEXTERAE

Toadflax, pennywort, mother of thousands,
Cymbalaria muralis ivy blooms
out the brick wall of a café garden.
Sunlit in the common era, it is late June
on Church Lane in Ledbury, Herefordshire,
and we have settled in for cakes and tea,
a bottle of designer lemonade—
Fentimans Natural, "Botanically Brewed,"
before we go to the poetry do.
Your fingers combing through the pink wallflowers,
you query the waitress, might she know the name—
these cymbal-shaped leaves, these wee snapdragons?
"Kenilworth ivy, wandering sailor;
it's everywhere and comes back every year."
The languor of your hand's loose scrutiny,
like a monk at a manuscript or a nun at beads,
or Adam naming animals and Eve,
or arching toward Creation's outstretched reach,
whilst lazing in the ceiling masterpiece:. . .
We weary of sorting the beauty of being.

MORNING AMONG PIEBALDS

This standing stillness among ruminants
inclines toward contemplations, perfectly
indifferent to a day's contingencies—
news of the world, some word on the weather—
and as for speaking to one another,
only insofar as communicants
extend their tongues, agape for Eucharist,
we yawn along a day's communion rail,
this presence, whether virtual or real,
we hunger after such companionships.
And so my piebald asses, lolling, move
in their haphazard unison as if
the hedge and greensward were their common table;
the silence hums a sort of reverence
for being and creation and the life
insouciant, still mindlessly alive.

BUSKERS

He reckoned she'd likely go for the busker
in Shop Street off Eyre Square with the topknot and sax—
a wastrel with waifish, world-weary good looks
he'd curl into a grin singing harmony with
the darkly fetching lead singer. She liked him too.
He imagined her making for the road with them,
maybe doing percussions and backup vocals,
city to city across the globe, the object
of their conjoined desires, Wendy to their lost boys,
a woman with lovers and cool allure,
such mysterious beauty to her being that
years after they'd still be whispering of it,
her lurid journals eventually published
in dozens of languages, all of them gold.

MEADOWHAWK

That late-summer red-bodied dragonfly,
the autumn meadowhawk, *Sympetrum vicinum*,
busy among the midgy hosta leaves
while squirrels high up in the walnut trees
let fall the soft green balls for winterage.
They plop all morning on the tarmacadam.
The world is hungry, craves, and stores and hoards,
though seldom notices enough's enough.
An image of the English Market, Cork,
and you among fresh fruits, green-groceries
fondling for readiness and ripening; the cheese-
monger's milky expertise—the blue, the brie,
the goat, this exquisite taleggio;
What next?—we pilgrims wonder—Where to go?

THE SICK OF THE PALSY HEALED AND
HIS SINS FORGIVEN

*Engraving by James Newton after Charles Reuben Ryley, 1795,
with gratitude for Heaney's "Miracle" in* Human Chain
Mark 2:1-12 KJV

The graver's title tells it in reverse.
So, which the greater miracle, we're asked,
to cleanse the soul or cure paralysis?
The mercy hidden or made manifest?
The King James version has forgiveness first,
the sins' remission quite invisible,
and then, to quiet the Scribes and Pharisees:
Arise! he says. Take up your bed and walk,
wherefore begrudgers and their begrudging talk
of blasphemy and sacrilege are hushed.
The palsied man stands up and saunters off,
bedroll and ropes gathered under his arm.
Behold, we never saw a thing like that!
The Savior's plain on this: it's faith that saves.
The boyos on the roof, like pallbearers
delivered of their corpse and coffin straps,
their thankless jobs, all heft and heave and lift,
done for yet another day, so they begin,
taking up their shovels, sods, and tiles,
to mend the mess they've made of it again.

BENEDICTION

for Corrine

I pray your eyes begin to well
the way mine do these latter years,
as pools of sadness and the joyous spill
over and into one another. Tears,
at how the young and beautiful all move
till there's no telling one from the other—
the wince, the grin, the grief, the gratitude,
their inter-coursing, grave embracing flesh,
fine edges blurred, love's wanting wound,
apposite, enraptured, confluent, bound;
Oh God, we say, in pleasure and in dread,
and God keeps silent so we carry on,
weeping, sighing, catching our breath
at seizures of being, at certain death.

So here's the pleading that I make for you:
May every moment and its opposite
move you to tears, as moments do,
till rheumy-eyed and lachrymal you slip
out of this veil, grace-filled, wide-eyed, spent,
beatific, consecrated, newly rent.

LITTLE ELEGY

for a dog who skipped out, and after X. J. Kennedy

Here lies loyal, trusted, true
friend for life, Bill W.,
named for Wordsworth and the guy
by whose twelve steps I've stayed dry,

sober even, these long years,
like the good dog buried here,
who could bark but never bit;
never strayed too far or shit

indoors; never fell from grace.
God, grant him this ground, this grave,
out of harm's way, ceaseless rest.
Of all good dogs, old Bill was best.

ACKNOWLEDGMENTS

When grievance and begrudgery threaten to overwhelm, the best of all bromides is gratitude. It is the lighter lift. So here is where I want to thank my agent and coconspirator, the late, lamented, and much beloved Richard P. McDonough—a bookish man who got this selection of poems settled in with Joshua Bodwell at the house of Godine just months before he joined the cloud of witnesses, those dead of blessed memory to whom this book, this bone rosary, endeavors to be a monument.

In addition, I'd like to thank the editors of the journals in which new poems in this collection first appeared: Colette Bryce at *Poetry Review* (UK); David Cooke at *The High Window* (UK); Eilean Ni Chuileanain and the late MacDara Woods at *Cyphers Magazine* in Dublin; Patrick Cotter at *Southword Journal* in Cork; Mary O'Donnell, of *The Stony Thursday Book* in Limerick; Jessie Lendennie at the *Salmon Anthology* in Galway; Gerard Smyth at the *Irish Times*; Monica Rico at *Bear River Review*; Jill Baumgaertner at *The Christian Century*; Don Share at *Poetry*, Brother Joe Hoover at *America Magazine*; Matt Boudway at *Commonweal*; Christopher Giroux, editor of the Roethke Calendar at Central Michigan University; and Shane McRae at *Image Magazine*, and Vivian Dorsel and Frances Richey at *upstreet Magazine*.

The scrutinies of John F. Nims, Gordon Lish, Robin Robertson, and Jill Bialosky have enriched this assemblage. I am grateful to them. And to Joshua Bodwell at Godine, whose close read and confidence have brought this book into being.

Likewise, these poems have benefited from the first readers and responders with whom I've shared new work over the past forty years, first among them Michael Heffernan, and in their own times, Keith Taylor, Richard Tillinghast, Julie Young, Mary Tata, Sean Lynch, Pat Lynch, Dan Lynch, George Martin, Emily Meier, Corrine Dagostino, and others, living and dead (the bed of heaven to them)—family, friends, and correspondents for whom my gratitude and indebtedness are permanent.

ABOUT THE AUTHOR

THOMAS LYNCH is the author of five books of essays, a book of short fiction, and five books of poetry. He was a National Book Award finalist for *The Undertaking: Life Studies from the Dismal Trade*, and has received the American Book Award, the Heartland Prize for Nonfiction, the Denise Levertov Award, the Great Lakes Book Award, and the Michigan Authors Award. He lives in Michigan—where, since 1973, he has been a funeral director—and in Ireland where he keeps an ancestral home.

A NOTE ON THE TYPE

Bone Rosary is set in Garamond. Our modern version was designed by Robert Slimbach, who based it on the typefaces created by the famed French printer Claude Garamond, a driving force behind typeface design during the sixteenth century. The oblique nature of the slimmest areas found in Garamond makes the typeface exceedingly graceful in print.

Book Design & Composition by Tammy Ackerman